"THE CONSTITUTION
OF THE PEOPLE"

"THE CONSTITUTION OF THE PEOPLE"

REFLECTIONS ON CITIZENS AND CIVIL SOCIETY

Edited by Robert E. Calvert

Introduction by Wilson Carey McWilliams

 UNIVERSITY PRESS OF KANSAS

© 1991 by the University Press of Kansas
Chapter 2 © by J. David Greenstone
Chapter 5 © by Michael Novak
All rights reserved

Published by the University Press of Kansas (Lawrence, Kansas 66045), which was organized
by the Kansas Board of Regents and is operated and funded by Emporia State University,
Fort Hays State University, Kansas State University, Pittsburg State University, the University
of Kansas, and Wichita State University

Library of Congress Cataloging-in-Publication Data

"The Constitution of the people": reflections on citizens and civil society
   / edited by Robert E. Calvert ; introduction by Wilson Carey
   McWilliams ; [contributors], J. David Greenstone . . . [et al.].
       p.   cm.
   Includes bibliographical references and index.
   ISBN 0-7006-0476-6 (alk. paper) — ISBN
0-7006-0478-2 (pbk.)
   1. Individualism.   2. Common good.   3. Political culture—United
States.   I. Calvert, Robert E.
JC571.U26   1991   90-48987
320.5 ' 12—dc20   CIP

British Library Cataloguing in Publication Data is available.

Printed in the United States of America
10 9 8 7 6 5 4 3 2 1

The paper used in this publication meets the minimum requirements of the American
National Standard for Permanence of Paper for Printed Library Materials Z39.48-1984.

To
David Greenstone
1937–1990

CONTENTS

THE CONTRIBUTORS

ROBERT N. BELLAH is Ford Professor of Sociology and Comparative Studies at the University of California at Berkeley.

ROBERT E. CALVERT is professor of political science at DePauw University.

JEAN BETHKE ELSHTAIN is the Centennial Professor of Political Science at Vanderbilt University.

The late J. DAVID GREENSTONE was William M. Benton Department Service Professor of Political Science at the University of Chicago.

WILSON CAREY MCWILLIAMS is professor of political science, Livingston College, Rutgers University.

MICHAEL NOVAK holds the George Frederick Jewett Chair in Religion and Public Policy at the American Enterprise Institute for Public Policy Research.

MICHAEL WALZER is on the permanent faculty of the Institute for Advanced Study.

PREFACE

This book was the idea of Richard F. Rosser, then president of De-
Pauw University, who asked me to plan a symposium here in the
spring of 1987. My charge was to select speakers whose lectures
might form a book that would honor both the Constitution and the
Sesquicentennial of the university's founding, which happened to
coincide with the Bicentennial of the Constitution. The actual
theme of the symposium—the meaning of membership in a constitutional order requiring political unity and committed to cultural
diversity—was inspired by DePauw's new president, Robert G. Bottoms, whose campaign to diversify the university in light of the
changing character of American society seemed to unite the two
commemorations. Prompted by this theme, the title of the book is
taken from a phrase of Thomas Paine's, who argued that the constitution of the people, their character as citizens and as a society, is
"antecedent" to the government formally established by a written
constitution.

The essays by Robert N. Bellah, J. David Greenstone, Michael
Novak, and Michael Walzer were originally delivered as lectures at
the symposium. Greenstone's and Novak's, as those present at the
event may recognize, are substantially revised versions of their lectures. The essays by Jean Bethke Elshtain and myself were written especially for this volume.

It is a pleasure to acknowledge the university's continued and un-
stinting support of this project, both the moral and financial support given at every turn by President Bottoms, the administrative
and clerical help provided by Associate Dean John White and his
most cooperative staff, the technical assistance offered by the people
in Media Services and in Academic Computing, and the resourceful
work of the reference librarians in the Roy O. West Library. I am indebted as well to the Dana Foundation for supporting three student
assistants, Douglas Driemeier, Donald Featherstone, and Vikash

Yadav, who as Dana Apprentices worked tirelessly and imaginatively with me on the editing of this volume and served as discerning critics in particular of my own essay. "Apprentices," they taught me as much as they learned.

I also wish to thank Director Fred Woodward and his able staff at the University Press of Kansas, for their wise advice and editorial talents as I encountered the problems, many of them new to me, associated with putting together a book of this kind. Special thanks are due Wilson Carey McWilliams, for his willingness to write an introduction for the book and for his many helpful editorial suggestions. Finally, the inevitable frustrations and sheer work associated with such a project were reduced enormously by the essayists themselves, who to a person met deadlines cheerfully and otherwise responded positively to the requests, some of them no doubt unreasonable or whimsical, of their editor.

Not the least of the rewards of serving as editor of this volume has been my good fortune in coming to know personally its several contributors. This is true above all of David Greenstone, who died, after a long illness, shortly after completing the final revision of his essay. My collaboration with David was especially close and intense, and in the course of many long letters and conversations, by telephone and in person, I came to appreciate and feel improved by his intellectual acuity, his compassionate wit, and the depth of his humanity. This book is dedicated to his memory.

Robert E. Calvert
Greencastle, Indiana
July, 1990

1
INTRODUCTION

WILSON CAREY MCWILLIAMS

> The Greeks thought of the polis as an active, formative thing, training the minds and characters of the citizens; we think of it as a piece of machinery for the production of safety and convenience. The training in virtue, which the medieval state left to the Church, and the polis made its own concern, the modern state leaves to God knows what.
>
> —*H. D. F. Kitto*

This book is an examination of American political life and culture by six distinguished scholars, an inquiry into our political soul that is urgently contemporary and mirrored in headlines.[1] At the same time, it speaks to the perennialities and, especially, to the political riddle of the many and the one.

All political societies are "many," complex unions of individuals and families, skills and interests, so that Aristotle regarded it as a decisive criticism of Plato's *Republic* that it seemed to reduce citizenship to a mere unison rather than a harmony.[2] Yet, just as harmony requires some ordering or ruling principle, every political society is also "one," identifiably different from all others, unique. The unity of a political society is thus tied to its identity, an understanding shared by its members of what collectively they are about, extended over time. It is not visible or material: Boundaries are drawn by convention or allegiance; and just as a nation like Poland can persist without "natural" frontiers, so geographic boundaries may enclose different and even hostile polities, as in Timor, Ireland, or Santo Domingo. The members of a public do not necessarily look very much alike, beyond the humanity that unites all peoples, nor are their material interests evidently common. Looking at any human group, the eye sees separate bodies; it may observe a physical similarity between members of families and clans; in villages and simple

1

societies it may even perceive common work, with a division of labor resting on age and gender, hinting at broadly similar interests. This is ordinary vision's outer limit. A political society, however, includes complexly related interests that often conflict; in these multinational days, moreover, citizens may very well have some interests that are closer to those of foreigners than to those of their fellows. For both reasons unity can be hard to discern. A political society can be symbolized, but it cannot be seen: It is defined by thought, reflected in speech and especially in law, so that "the one" is ultimately an idea, a quality of spirit that serves as the rule or measure for the quantities that we see in political life.[3] Thus American patriotism, in Adlai Stevenson's noble evocation: "When an American says that he loves his country, he means not only that he loves the New England hills, the prairies glistening in the sun, the wide and rising plains, the great mountains and the sea. He means that he loves an inner air, an inner light in which freedom lives and in which a man can draw the breath of self-respect."[4] These essays are explorations in political interiority, an attempt to answer Kitto's question, united by the effort to understand the identity of the United States in a way that does justice to the paradoxes and pluralities of American politics.

The book opens with J. David Greenstone's description of American political culture as a continuing debate between two contending versions of liberal democracy; Robert N. Bellah and Jean Bethke Elshtain then offer diagnoses of the condition of civil society in America, based on their understandings of the relation between individuality and community; Michael Novak and Michael Walzer present two very different views of the Constitution and its impact on American life; finally, Robert E. Calvert ties his analysis of the Progressive tradition to a challenging delineation of the language and conduct of modern American politics. Each essay has its own special sound, and there is more than a little discord: Michael Novak is less critical of American life than the other contributors and more inclined to see economics as a cornerstone of republican government; in a more muted way, Jean Bethke Elshtain worries about the implications of some of her colleagues' appreciation of community. But for all their jangling, these essays have an assonance and, perhaps, a melody.

As Robert Bellah observes, *e pluribus unum*, the republic's motto, originally referred to the states and the federal government, political societies within a larger union, but that relationship is otherwise all but invisible in this book. In our America, national institutions and allegiances have overwhelmed the states, and the contributors to this volume seem content to have it so, although several express regret at the decline of the local and participant politics that Tocqueville admired. In these essays, "the many" ordinarily refers to individuals or to the families, churches, and associations of "civil society," distinguished from the State. With varying emphasis, all the contributors warn against the abuse and overextension of State power. An even stronger theme, however, is set by Tocqueville's fear that individualism, having undermined political life, eventually would weaken all relationships, leaving human beings only so many isolated selves, creatures of the moment, desperate but trivial.[5] And all these essays seek some *tertium*, some middle term between a State grown too intrusive and citizens become too distant from public life, a balance between particular freedom and common purpose.

To speak of purpose is to recall Aristotle's argument that every regime, every "constitution," rests on an implicit answer to the question, "What is the good life?" As Robert Calvert suggests in the concluding essay, Americans from the beginning have assumed a close relationship between their own prospects for a good life and the Constitution bestowed by the founders and ordained by their predecessors. And this is the fundamental basis of paradox and ambiguity in our own time.

Augustine's grand simplification of Aristotle's question, and our own, reduced the answers to two: "self-love reaching the point of contempt for God" contrasted with "the love of God carried as far as contempt for self." Recognizing that, in secular practice, no person and no regime is wholly devoted to one or the other of these warring principles in the human soul, Augustinian doctrine regards all politics as a struggle for preeminence between the two loves and their two cities.[6]

In the American tradition, this is a familiar dialectic, the basis of a "people of paradox," wonderfully captured by David Greenstone's contrast of the "two liberalisms" of Jefferson and Adams and the "civic ambivalence" they entail.[7] Their modern teachers—primarily Locke and his epigones—taught and teach Americans to see human beings as by nature separate individuals, so many bodies, each with its desires and private experiences, engrossed with the pursuit of gratification and self-preservation. Political society, in these terms, is an instrument for affording a more effective individual liberty through civil peace and the mastery of nature. The "first object of government," Madison urged, is to preserve and enable a fuller development of our diverse faculties.[8] Consequently, the common good is only an aggregate in which, at any point, some will be losers; a more inclusive version of the public interest requires that government be so contrived that the "silent operation of the laws" guarantees, in the long term, a measure of equality and community (an unlikely result, Greenstone observes, when some of the losers were slaves.)[9]

By contrast, dominant religions in the United States have taught that originally, individuals are not free. The body, left to itself, is slavish, the prisoner of desire, while the soul's self-centered, inward rejection of its finitude, dependence, and mortality is a denial of its very humanity, not liberty but illusion. Redemption in the highest sense may be the work of Grace. Nevertheless, biblical religion in America has generally assigned a role to human societies and polities in drawing the self out of its sullen privacies.[10] Shrewdly used, delight, punishment, and the regulation of ambition can attach individuals to family, property, friends, country, and even, more tenuously, to humanity itself, nurturing the human capacity for love. In this view, "self-determining power" (John Adams's phrase) is developed only through communities which help us to govern impulse and overcome illusion. Even the highest liberty, beyond the reach of convention and law, belongs to citizens of God's city, who see the partiality of all human polities and things. Individuality is antithetical to individualism, and loving sacrifice for the common good is the expression of a free spirit.

Greenstone argues persuasively that a healthy politics in America requires a balanced dialogue between these historic voices, a skeptical individualism to guard against rigidity and dogma, and a reformed, transcendent doctrine to regulate individual and group selfishness. But maintaining such a balance is a difficult task calling for great statecraft and good fortune. The ordinary rule when first principles conflict, as Lincoln observed in relation to slavery, is that a house divided cannot stand; a riven regime must dissolve or move toward coherence, a new unity based on the victory of one side or the triumph of a higher standard capable of subordinating the older antagonisms.[11] In any viable political society, the one must enfold and govern the many.[12]

In their different ways, all the contributors to this book worry that the religious, communitarian voice in America's cultural debate is growing dangerously reedy, increasingly inaudible against a strident individualism. Robert Bellah and Jean Elshtain make explicit appeals to Catholic social teaching and to Protestant thinkers like Reinhold Niebuhr and Glenn Tinder; Walzer, Calvert, and Greenstone invoke republican values informed by religion. Even Michael Novak, who celebrates the Framers' interest in commercial enterprise, urges us to see commerce as the foundation of their republicanism, part of a *political* design devoted to the inventive and creative spirit, not merely the private pursuit of material gain—a grand adventure rather than a sordid scrabbling.

These concerns are at least as old as the Constitution, the echo of Anti-Federalist warnings against the neglect of public spirit and moral virtue. As Novak reminds us, the American Framers, devoted to individual liberty, rejected the prevailing aristocratic ideal of a virtuous republic, abandoning the effort to overcome the "causes" of a factious private spirit—impossible without intolerable repression, or so Madison claimed in *Federalist* 10—in favor of controlling its "effects." In that familiar argument, the danger of majority faction, the chief problem of republican government, is minimized by a large republic in which majorities will necessarily be shifting coalitions, full of conflict and based on compromise, morally mediocre at best. For the Framers, it counted as an advantage that such a politics teaches citizens to limit their political commitments and enthusiasms: In the school of *The Federalist*, detachment substitutes for civic virtue.

In the Framers' doctrine, attachment is to be distrusted because the ties of love and community bind individuals to particular places and persons, institutions, and ideas without regard to their utility. It makes matters worse that the strongest attachments, the results of early education and long familiarity, chain us to the past.[13] Even reason is dangerous when reinforced by attachment. Like human beings themselves, Madison argues, human reason is "timid and cautious when left alone, and acquires firmness and confidence in proportion to the number with which it is associated."[14] In association, human beings are apt to reason and act boldly, and at moments like the American Revolution, when private passions are restrained by common danger and shared outrage, an empowered citizenry may become a fraternal public, capable of great things. The Framers, however, had little more fondness than Jean Elshtain for such "armed virtue," especially since they thought it certain to be short lived. Under ordinary circumstances, they held that individuals are likely to be more rational in isolation. Leaders who are subject to scrutiny and hopeful of honor may be able to discipline private desires; for most citizens, the combination of personal invisibility with strength of numbers is an invitation to faction and partisanship. Even if every Athenian citizen had been a Socrates,

Madison contended, the Athenian assembly would have been a mob.[15]

The Framers hoped that the large republic and the Constitution's design would leave individuals free but psychologically detached, experiencing within civil society a gentle version of the vulnerability of the state of nature, with its impetus for order. Human beings who are "left alone" reason timidly, their very fearfulness a check on passion. They are apt to be circumspect, and to that extent, public-regarding, watching and keeping up the appearances and inclined to be decently law-abiding.

As Novak's account suggests, commerce is a centerpiece in this plan for public peace through detachment, since the national market frees and tames, stimulating ambition but broadening and disciplining avarice, and forcing at least a consideration of other interests. Moreover, since values vary with supply and demand, commercial life promotes flexibility, an emotional detachment from any particular products or relationships, and especially, a responsiveness to public opinion. Subtly, these economic lessons also assail prejudice and hint that all virtues and faiths are only so many relativities, commodities for exchange.[16]

Certainly, commerce was one of the tempters intended to wean Americans away from attachment to the states. To the Framers, surely to Hamilton, if less clearly to Madison, the states, like all political societies, were only artifacts created to advance the interests of individuals and had become essentially outdated, parochial obstacles to opportunity supported by habit and affection. Consequently, the Constitution allows the federal government to exert its powers directly on individuals, so that it may make a claim on "those passions which have the strongest influence upon the human heart."[17] In the Framers' view, it is natural for interest to prevail unless confused and opposed by overwhelming attachment; by breaking into "those channels and currents in which the passions of mankind naturally flow," federal power allows interest to make itself felt. Better administered—or so the Framers trusted—and able to hold out the lures of wealth and power, the central government and national life could be expected to detach affections from the states.[18] It did not trouble the Framers greatly that the national regime would attract only diffuse affections and relatively weak attachments: Lukewarm patriotism, like timid reason, suits a government intended to be the servant of individual liberty.

This is not the only way the work of the American founders can be understood. Hannah Arendt claimed that the basis of the Constitution was a new and distinctively American understanding of power, power that both Madison and Hamilton sought to harness and control, if for different purposes.[19] The political machinery they created was both "meant to be powerful," as Walzer notes, and also grounded in the people, with their "passions" not diminished but properly channeled through relatively virtuous representatives. And Bellah elsewhere argues that Madison himself had not wholly given up on popular republican virtue.[20]

The Founders surely recognized the need for some sort of moral and civic virtue as the foundation for the republic's laws and liberties. Just as self-preservation does not inspire citizens to risk their lives in defense of their country, the interests of individuals do not necessarily incline them to fulfill their contracts or obey the law, especially if they are poor, obscure, or oppressed, combining desperation with some hope of going unnoticed. And in general, the founding generation regarded religion, broadly defined, as an indispensable element of moral education. Even the enlightened Jefferson preferred the social teaching of Jesus over the privatism of Epicurus, whom he otherwise admired. Thinkers like Adams excepted, however, the leading spirits among the Founders tended to see moral indoctrination as a benign deception, practiced on behalf of the community's "aggregate interests" on individuals whose reason was unreliable, or on those — most evidently, slaves, as Bellah indicates — whose very rights and interests were violated by the law. In these terms, moral and religious education teaches a combination of useful untruths or half-truths — that one should never tell a lie, for example, or that promises should always be kept — and propositions that are far from certain, like the doctrine that a Supreme Judge will detect and punish all crimes and reward all virtues that are neglected here below.[21]

Politically necessary, moral education is at least questionable in the Framers' theory, a kind of sharp practice too dangerous to be trusted to government and also demeaning for a regime devoted to individual freedom and reasoned consent. Consequently, most of the founding generation were content to leave the shaping of character to families and churches, to civil society, and in some cases, to the states; and Walzer is right to note that the founders relied on groups strong and stable enough to nurture conscientious souls. "Our constitution," John Adams declared, "was made only for a moral and religious people. It is wholly inadequate to the government of any other."[22] At the same time, however, the Framers gave these groups no constitutional status or notice: The Constitution acknowledges no subjects other than persons and states. While left largely at liberty, civil society and local community were subordinated to a constitution — and through it, to a national market — whose ruling principle is individual freedom, advanced by the strategy of detachment. From the beginning, the laws have worked to undermine the "habits of the heart."

Nevertheless, in contemporary America, this long-term tendency has taken on a magnitude so great as to resemble a change of kind, like pebbles become an avalanche: Perceptively, Walzer speaks of a second Constitution, a virtually new regime, Calvert of Progressivism's politically denatured citizen. Tocqueville's Americans, for all their "taste for well-being," were at least familiar with the biblical and republican languages of the common good.[23] Today, as Robert Bellah has indicated, even public-spirited Americans — a more significant group than we sometimes imagine — are more and more inclined to justify their lives and deeds in terms of calculating self-interest ("utilitarian individualism") or personal authenticity ("expressive individualism").[24] To a surprisingly wide public, it is now axiomatic that moral and political norms are relative to one's times or culture, the reflection of the unique experience of individuals or groups, and perhaps the strongest intellectual current of the day regards speech itself as only a construction for private purposes, an instrument for domination.[25] The revived "discussion concerning political philosophy," to which Bellah invites Americans, requires us to recover or learn the power of public speech.

However, curing political aphonia is not easy, and Robert Calvert's shrewd diagnosis indicates some of the difficulties and the dangers. He argues that in their effort to develop a new public philosophy and a language of politics suited to modern America, Progressive theorists found it necessary to challenge the authority of the Framers and that of the "steel chain" of nineteenth-century orthodoxy. Following Beard's "debunking" of the high claims of the founding, Progressivism developed an "anti-myth" to take the place of the traditional American democrat, describing politics not as an affair of citizens but as nothing more than a conflict of interests, a parallelogram of forces. Paradoxically, however, the upshot of this Progressive critique has been to strengthen but vulgarize the Framers' emphasis on self-interest. Retaining the belief that political society is a contrivance manufactured to serve private aims, Progressive doctrine denied the Framers' claim that a political minority may act from broader and more elevated ideas of self, identifying with the polities it creates or governs, or even with humankind.[26] But if Progressive teaching acted a democratic part in "unmasking" the pretensions of the elite, it also stripped away the moral claim of the many: Justice, Progressive analysis implied, is the interest of the stronger, and any appeal to a public or common good is only the rationalization of subjective interests and values.[27] Deemphasizing speech, Progressivism imitated and extended the Framers' reliance on political technology, hoping to make good the deficiencies of the Constitution's "mechanistic" politics through a more "organic" social science and a more scientific administration.

Yet whatever their faults, the Progressives were wrestling with problems that still shadow our politics, most notably the republic's setbacks in its struggles with power. As Novak indicates, the American Founders accepted a considerable measure of inequality as the natural expression of individual differences, the social and economic face of personality. On the other hand, the Founders also recognized that unequal wealth and power can be used to restrict the development of the faculties of the disadvantaged.[28] For a solution, they relied on the "silent operation of the laws," hoping that the advantage they saw in a large republic—the competition between many interests, denying more than short-term ascendancy to any—would be an effective check on inequality in social and economic life as well as in politics.[29] It didn't work: Large-scale private organizations largely elude those controls, and many have come to constitute private governments on which citizens depend and to which, for practical purposes, they can create no alternative.[30] Private power called for public government in its own image, and that necessity—reinforced by international politics and by technology—has created a politics dominated by mass associations and great bureaucracies, aggregations of money, technique, and support adequate to the scale and intricacy of modern life.

Necessarily, this sort of politics grows away from most citizens, losing its connection to their daily lives and competences. It is now almost axiomatic that organizations large enough to be politically effective will dwarf their individual members.[31] *Public* politics, the sphere of speech and deliberation, has come to seem less and less relevant or worthy of attention. In the mass media, the coverage of what candidates say, never very extensive, is losing ground to an analysis of their advertisements, now treated as news events, while the content of either kind of statement is given less attention than the strategy it reflects. The "real world" of politics increasingly is presented and understood as outside the public's view, a place of bureaucrats and hidden persuaders, penetrable only by experts.[32] For too many Americans, the political is a place of indignity, where they are not heard and do not matter—except as parts of some abstract, statistical category—and in which they are subject to manipulation and deception. Small wonder that private life engrosses Americans, or that the republic suffers from a chronic shortage of public confidence and commitment.[33]

However, the private order—civil society—is itself in disarray. Limited liability, the great capitalist principle, seems to permeate social life. Divorce, as a normal and even expected hazard, teaches Americans to be at least guarded in their commitments. Even stable families, none too numerous, are likely to be short-term associations for limited purposes, composed of only two generations and pressed to find "quality time."[34] Local communities, vulnerable to change, are also weakened by mobility, and the loss of old homes and friends counsels us to be content with superficial roots and relationships. Associational life grows more peripheral, displaced by private recreations and a politics in which the donation of money, solicited by mail or phone, is replacing membership in face-to-face groups as the reigning mode of civic participation.[35] It is an "unconstituted" society the citizen must vainly try to face.

The extent of this privatization is debatable, and Elshtain warns against exaggerating it; but the problem is serious and the tendency alarming. All the contributors to this book are broadly Aristotelian in regarding civil society, though formally separate from the state, as playing an indispensable role in the regime, particularly as the first course in civic edification, the traditional school and stronghold of communitarian teaching. Thus their evident conviction, Aristotelian through and through, that the American Constitution must ultimately be judged by the "way of life" it reflects and encourages. At the same time, they recognize that civil society cannot be self-ruling. Households and other social groups, Aristotle argued, nurture and provide for individuals, aiming at the safeguarding of "mere life." Beyond the securing of physical existence, however, families and associations require some other rule and principle: Even the enrichment of material life depends on the division of labor and the exchange of products, and hence, on political institutions like money.[36] An association like the market or the church, the community theater or the professional society, enhances our lives in some respect, but a fully human environment depends on access to all these associations and hence on political principles and institutions which assign to each its place and its limits. As Bellah indicates, without a common rule, pluralism degenerates into communalism—Lebanon's agony—or into the less stark, but more radical, fragmentations of individualism.

Of course, there is not much doubt as to which is the greater danger in the United States: The Constitution and the laws accentuate or promote the weakening of civil society. As Walzer observes, the Constitution affords Americans any number of ways to exit from relationships, localities, and social institutions, but the voice it gives them to work for the improvement of groups and communities is rarely as loud as a whisper in the din of modern politics and economics. Public life and spirit suffer, since it is easier to leave a city than combat its decay, and in contemporary constitutional law, Walzer points out, rights to exit or separate have become "a virtual substitute for social change." Even decency is hard-pressed: "The scale and dynamism of American democracy," Lewis Lapham writes, "grants the ceaselessly renewable option of moving one's conscience into a more congenial street."[37] By contrast, both Walzer and Elshtain ask for what amounts to a civil revolution, a public policy which cherishes the solidarities of civil society, lending the support of law to the internal life and cohesion of associations, hoping—as Elshtain puts it—to strengthen moral obligations rather than substitute for them.

Of course, none of the authors in this book needs to be reminded that communities and social groups can be repressive, or that they can tear up, as well as lay down, the foundations of human excellence. They expect government to protect civil rights and to regulate groups by the standard of public purpose; the doctrine of subsidiarity, which Elshtain derives from Catholic thought, subordinates civil society and yet respects its sphere. However, Walzer speaks for the contributors—Novak excepted, at least in part—when he urges Americans and American law to see rights as the basis of politics rather than private immunities, less as barriers against government than as claims to government of a certain kind. The soul needs the city: Human beings are certainly political animals, if they are also something more, and citizenship is the middle term between individuals and individuality. In this view, American democracy should be understood as a form of "associated living," in John Dewey's phrase, a way of life entitled to rule private liberties and gratifications.

There is in these essays, then, at least the outline of an answer to Kitto's vital question. For Novak it is commerce (but not only commerce) that must train us in the virtue enabling us to be unified as well as diverse and industrious. The remaining authors are more or less Tocquevillian, preferring to believe that the "political associations" of civil society may yet serve to some degree as "large free schools" in which we may learn the arts of association in general. There is no nostalgia in these essays for the glory that was the ancient city-state nor even for a fabled and simpler American past; the necessity, in Bellah's precise formulation, is for a "critical reappropriation" of our political and religious traditions. Rather, the essays aim at the recovery—or the reappreciation—of republican politics, a prescription less for a polity conceived as an engine of virtue militant than for one no longer able to aspire to unchecked dominion.

This is a contemporary version of the ancient argument that a republic must prefer political freedom to affluence, treating its liberties as beyond price, so that in principle it must always suspect wealth and subject it to limits.[38] Through much of its history, America has felt able to evade that choice and necessity, favored as the country has been by nature, culture and situation. Today, however, the embattled economy of the United States needs the disciplines of self-denial, the ethics of craft and saving no longer adequately supported by "worldly asceticism."[39] Even economic well-being, in our time, calls for some sacrifice of personal comfort and immediate desire on the altar of common purpose.

For all their diversity, these essays share a regard for America's political institutions—the common ground, as Greenstone notes, for the very different liberalisms of Jefferson and Adams. And at least a majority of the contributors are convinced that America faces a time of great decisions, calling for great politics. Like the hope of rearticulating the second, communitarian voice of the American tradition, the plea for reinvigorated public discussion—Elshtain's "fractious" politics—runs through the book like a leitmotif.

There is a connection between Royce's *Philosophy of Loyalty*, invoked by Bellah, and the special role of political parties in democratic deliberation, as competitive subcommunities which are also self-consciously parts of a political whole.[40] The arguments in this book give support to the effort to renew political parties, particularly local party organizations as opposed to national bureaucracies. Yet each of the essayists has his or her own preferred schools of political speech and allegiance. Walzer suggests that "state action" in the service of democracy, public policy aimed at encouraging the solidarities necessary to republican politics (he cites the Wagner Act), is hardly unprecedented. We should be willing to listen to all such suggestions. Animating political debate is almost desperately difficult, but events are pressing Americans to discover to what extent they still speak a common language.

For more than fifty years, foreign policy has substituted for public philosophy, establishing the United States as the champion of freedom in its contest with totalitarianism. That stark confrontation justified departures from democratic practice and the imperial expansion of executive prerogative. It also seemed to justify the regime as a whole, since America's faults, even serious ones, were less severe than those of her rivals: To a great many Americans, any faultfinding was morally obtuse, not to say unpatriotic, while others, more tolerant, treated criticism as "idealism," mere word-spinning, irrelevant to the real struggles of the real world. Of course, foreign policy sometimes moved America in the direction of reform: The need to blunt the appeals of communism, here and abroad, was an important argument in favor of greater racial and economic equality. Nevertheless, Americans have been encouraged and accustomed to see domestic political life in the scenes and costumes of the international megadrama.

With the waning of the cold war, anticommunism is losing its force as a negative public purpose, and the United States has an opportunity to look inward, to mend or reweave the fabric of law and society. A half-century of habits, however, is not easily put aside, especially since it is tempting to fix on the fear of enemies when the sources of civic trust and affection run thin. Elshtain's critique of "armed virtue," consequently, is an invaluable and pointed lesson (one paralleled, in domestic life, by Bellah's dissection of "communalist pluralism"). A country—or a soul—defined by negation is not autonomous: It is the mirror of its antagonist, ruled by the contest it hopes to win. Hatred of enemies asks too little of friends.

Historically, American xenophobia has always been at least troubled by the universalism of religion and natural right. In Sam Adams's vision of the virtuous city, Boston, like Winthrop's city on a hill, was to be a *Christian* Sparta, austere but humble, patriotic but aware of the duty to love peace and show compassion.[41]

Less certain in faith, contemporary Americans still profess a belief in the proposition that all human beings are created equal; that bedrock of our nationality is a starting point for reconstruction. An antidote to individualism, equality links us to others: We can be free alone, but it is only in relationships that we can be equal or have rights. Equality also opposes relativism, since it argues that our common humanity is decisive, a quality that overrides all others, a likeness that makes one of many. By implication, all cultures and

polities are not incommensurable, but variations on a theme, answers, more or less adequate, to the human dilemma. Equality, G.
K. Chesterton observed, sets limits and duties, so that America turns
on "the pure classic conception that no man must aspire to be anything more than a citizen, and that no man shall endure to be anything less."[42] For all their different accents, these essays speak the
language of the universal, seeking to recall America to its best and
ancient creed.

NOTES

1. Michael Oreskes, "America's Politics Loses Way as Its Vision Changes
World," *New York Times*, 18 March 1990, pp. 1ff.

2. Aristotle *Politics* 1261a17–1261b33. In fact, excepting some indivisible monad, all things are "many," comprising various parts and qualities
(Plato *Republic* 476a).

3. *Politics* 1252b28–1253a38.

4. "The Nature of Patriotism," speech to the American Legion Convention, New York City, 27 August 1952, in *The Papers of Adlai E. Stevenson*,
ed. W. Johnson (Boston and Toronto: Little, Brown, 1974), 4:53.

5. Alexis de Tocqueville, *Democracy in America*, trans. George Lawrence, ed. J. P. Mayer (Garden City, N.Y.: Doubleday, 1969), 2: bk. 2,
chap. 2.

6. *Politics* 1252a1–8; Augustine, *The City of God*, trans. Henry S. Bet-
tenson (Baltimore: Penguin Books, 1984), bk. 14, chaps. 1, 28.

7. Michael Kammen, *People of Paradox* (New York: Knopf, 1972).

8. *Federalist* 10. On Locke's influence, and that of modern political philosophy generally, see Thomas Pangle, *The Spirit of Modern Republicanism* (Chicago: University of Chicago Press, 1988), and Steven Dworetz, *The
Unvarnished Doctrine* (Durham, N.C.: Duke University Press, 1990).

9. *The Writings of James Madison*, ed. G. Hunt, 6 vols. (New York: Putnam, 1900–1910), 6:86.

10. Cf. Jean Elshtain's view of Christianity and the body on p. 70.

11. The rise of the secular state, elevating civil peace over religious
unity, is the obvious example of the successful assertion of a new principle
of rule. In the slavery controversy, Judge Douglas attempted to make "popular sovereignty" into a superordinate law, following the logic of Locke's description of the state of nature (*Second Treatise of Government*, ed.
Thomas P. Reardon [New York: Macmillan, 1986], par. 96.) We are fortunate that, in this case, the appeal of pragmatic accommodation was a failure. See Harry V. Jaffa, *Crisis of the House Divided* (Seattle: University of
Washington Press, 1973).

12. Contemporary "nonfoundationalists" often argue that, in the ab-
sence of any ground for preferring one view to another, tolerance ought to

prevail. But this view, of course, actually asserts toleration as a *grundnorm*. As Michael Sandel writes, liberal values "can hardly be defended by the claim that no values can be defended" ("Morality and the Liberal Ideal," *New Republic* 190 [7 May 1984], 15).

13. Madison maintained that ancient "examples," most obviously religion, double the strength of opinion (*Federalist* 49). Americans are admirable because they have not allowed "a blind veneration for antiquity, for custom or for names" to outweigh their good sense and experience (*Federalist* 14). But all customary attachment tends to be blind: When Madison refers to the veneration "which time bestows on everything," his observation indicates how indiscriminate such reverence is. Such authority may "perhaps" be necessary to the stability of a free government, and the support of prejudice will not be "superfluous," but Madison will not go beyond these very limited, grudging concessions (*Federalist* 49).

14. *Federalist* 49.

15. *Federalist* 55.

16. The broadening effect of commerce is indicated by Hamilton's argument that the "extensive inquiry and observation" of merchants makes them the natural patrons of manufacturers and tradesmen (*Federalist* 35). On detachment and the moral effects of commerce, see Ralph Lerner, "Benjamin Franklin: Spectator," in *The Thinking Revolutionary* (Ithaca, N.Y.: Cornell University Press, 1987), pp. 41–59, and Thomas Pangle, *Montesquieu's Philosophy of Liberalism* (Chicago: University of Chicago Press, 1973), pp. 200–248, or consider Hobbes's echoing reduction of human worth to one's price, "a thing dependant on the need and judgement of another" (*Leviathan*, chap. 10).

17. *Federalist* 16.

18. *Federalist* 27; see also *Federalist* 17 and 24.

19. See Hannah Arendt, *On Revolution* (New York: Viking, 1965), pp. 165–67.

20. See Robert Bellah et al., *Habits of the Heart* (Berkeley and Los Angeles: University of California Press, 1985), pp. 253–54.

21. Nathan Tarcov, *Locke's Education for Liberty* (Chicago: University of Chicago Press, 1984), p. 182. For example, Franklin held that a belief in "particular Providence" is necessary to "weak and ignorant Men and Women, and . . . inexperienc'd and inconsiderate Youth of both Sexes" (*Benjamin Franklin: Writings*, ed. J. A. Leo Lemay [New York: Library of America, 1987], p. 748).

22. John Adams, "Reply to the Massachusetts Militia," 11 October 1789, cited in John R. Howe, *The Changing Political Thought of John Adams* (Princeton, N.J.: Princeton University Press, 1966), p. 185.

23. *Democracy in America*, 2: bk. 1, chap. 5, and bk. 2, chap. 15 (although see also bk. 2, chap. 9).

24. Bellah et al., *Habits of the Heart*.

25. Most critics appear to have conceded Allan Bloom's observation re-

garding relativism's reigning status among students (*The Closing of the American Mind* [New York: Simon and Schuster, 1987], p. 25), contenting themselves with the response that relativism is either unthreatening or a correct attitude.

26. On the Framers' view, see David Epstein, *The Political Theory of the Federalist* (Chicago: University of Chicago Press, 1984).

27. In the same way, as Eric Goldman observed, in the effort to overcome Social Darwinism, Progressives developed a "reform Darwinism" that insisted on the relativity of all institutions, undermining their opponents but cutting the moral ground from under their own feet (*Rendezvous with Destiny* [New York: Knopf, 1953]). On "debunking" as an intellectual mode, see Karl Mannheim, *Freedom, Power and Democratic Planning* (New York: Oxford University Press, 1950), pp. 295–97.

28. *The Papers of James Madison*, ed. W. T. Hutchinson et al., (Chicago: University of Chicago Press, 1962–), 9:76.

29. *Writings of James Madison*, 6:86.

30. Grant McConnell, *Private Power and American Democracy* (New York: Knopf, 1966).

31. Karl Mannheim, *Man and Society in an Age of Reconstruction* (New York: Harcourt Brace, 1951), pp. 97–98.

32. Todd Gitlin, "The Candidate Factory," *Boston Review* (August 1988), pp. 6, 23; John Kenneth Galbraith, "Coolidge, Carter, Bush, Reagan," *New York Times*, 12 December 1988, sec. A, p. 16.

33. Seymour Martin Lipset and William Schneider, *The Confidence Gap* (New York: Free Press, 1983).

34. Judith S. Wallerstein and Sandra Blakeslee, *Second Chances* (New York: Ticknor and Fields, 1989); Christopher Lasch, *Haven in a Heartless World* (New York: Basic Books, 1977).

35. The recognition of this fact is the one sound element in the Court's opinion in Buckley v. Valeo, 424 U.S. 1 (1976).

36. *Politics* 1257a31–1257b1. *Nomisma* (money) derives from *nomos* (law): See Ernest Barker's Introduction to *Politics* (Oxford: Clarendon, 1952), p. lxx.

37. "Notebook: Supply-Side Ethics," *Harper's* 270 (May 1985), p. 11.

38. Hence the Anti-Federalists, though far from ascetic, declaimed against "luxury," and Thomas Jefferson worried that the people would "forget themselves, but in the sole faculty of making money," losing the ability to act politically to achieve a "due respect for their rights" (*Life and Selected Writings of Thomas Jefferson*, ed. A. Koch and W. Peden [New York: Modern Library, 1944], p. 277).

39. The phrase, of course, is from Max Weber, *The Protestant Ethic and the Spirit of Capitalism* (New York: Scribner, 1958).

40. Joel Silbey, *The Partisan Imperative* (New York: Oxford University Press, 1985).

41. *The Writings of Samuel Adams*, ed. H. Cushing (New York: Putnam, 1908), 4:238.

42. G. K. Chesterton, *What I Saw in America* (New York: Dodd Mead, 1922), p. 16.

2

ADAMS AND JEFFERSON ON SLAVERY: TWO LIBERALISMS AND THE ROOTS OF CIVIC AMBIVALENCE

J. DAVID GREENSTONE

The Declaration of Independence and the Constitution affirm the vision of *e pluribus unum*. While promising "a more perfect union," they also committed the United States to the essentials of liberal politics: limited government, individual rights, and (eventually) political equality. One influential interpretation holds that Americans have been liberal to a fault. We have avoided political and social fragmentation only by adopting a deep and abiding cultural consensus, and this single liberal ideology has effectively precluded any meaningful disagreement over fundamental—that is, philosophical—issues. The price of our admittedly enviable political stability, therefore, has been an individualism masquerading as "diversity" and a stifling uniformity, indeed a "tyranny," of mass opinion, a caricature of genuine political unity.[1]

This claim bears directly on the question of unity and diversity in American life. As I have argued elsewhere, it is partially, but quite seriously, mistaken.[2] American politics, I contend, has been *pervasively* liberal, but not *consensually* so. For at least a century and a half, it has been marked by a conflict between two very different liberal traditions over a range of essentially philosophical questions. On one side, a *humanist* liberalism has emphasized individuals as holders of preferences that must in principle be respected equally

This essay benefited from the criticism and comments of Chris Ansell, Robert Calvert, Louisa Bertch Green, Carla Hess, John Schlotterbeck, and Vickie Sullivan.

and ought in practice to be satisfied as equitably as possible. On the other side, to adopt the terminology of Franklin Gamwell, a *reformed*, originally neo-Calvinist liberalism has emphasized individual faculties that ought actively to be cultivated, often in and through political action.[3] The chief duty is to develop the abilities of oneself and one's fellow citizens. There are profound implications for our politics and political culture in the conflict between these two liberalisms, it seems to me, that the standard theory of liberalism either ignores or misunderstands.

When we view American liberalism as bipolar, we see that our unity is not simple but complex, marked as it is by agreement on some beliefs and divergence on others. Accordingly, I believe this bipolarity is as much a source of cultural diversity as are differences based on religion, race, ethnicity, or gender. Precisely because this diversity derives from so fundamental a tension in our basic political culture, it conditions the ways we deal with other cultural differences in our politics. I want to suggest, finally, that the tension between our two liberalisms, and our sometimes fitful attempts to embrace both, engenders a deep ambivalence both about our personal responsibilities as citizens and about our ethical responsibilities as members of the American community.

To provide a foundation for this claim, I shall examine the thought and politics of John Adams and Thomas Jefferson, the two great revolutionary figures on diplomatic service in 1787 who assumed leading roles under the newly ratified Constitution. As I shall try to show, for all Jefferson's egalitarian fervor, his humanist liberalism readily supported the protective attitude toward slavery that he eventually adopted. In contrast, however conservative his own inclinations, Adams's reformed liberalism readily supported his own and, much more, his family's antislavery inclinations.

Before developing this account in detail, a word is in order about procedures and assumptions. First, while noting both their many common convictions and their political disagreements, I mainly want to connect Adams's and Jefferson's specifically philosophic differences to the slavery issue that would engulf their successors. Second, I want to examine the consequences of this connection for the outlooks of their followers, in order to illuminate central features of American political thought and culture. I advance no claim here that their philosophic orientations had a direct or singularly determining influence on the political cleavages of later decades, or for that matter even of their own. At best, Jefferson's humanist liberalism made it easier for most, but not all, of his northern followers to seek an accommodation with the slave states. So too, Adams's reformed liberalism made it easier for many, though not all, of those who shared his ethical commitments to give increasing support to the antislavery cause.

Instead, I shall treat these beliefs not as causes but as *dispositions*, that is, combinations of concepts and attitudes that encourage certain types of reactions to particular events but discourage others. Such a triggering or genuinely causal event might be an important economic or social change, for example, slavery's growing importance in the southern economy. Given this change, the presence of opposed dispositions helps account for the ensuing heightened conflict. Specifically, I shall argue that the two liberalisms of Jefferson and Adams permitted and even encouraged just such conflicting responses to slavery's changing status. In that sense their debates show Jefferson and Adams to be *revealing* rather than representative or fundamentally innovative intellectual figures. Though not great philosophers, they nevertheless went beyond their conventional countrymen in delineating the conceptual and normative resources available in their humanist and reformed liberalisms. Thus they illuminated the ground on which the battle over slavery would be fought in the next generation, as well as later cleavages in American politics.

ADAMS, JEFFERSON, AND THE SLAVERY ANOMALY

"I have thus stated my opinion on a point on which we differ," Thomas Jefferson wrote John Adams in 1813, "not with a view to controversy, for we are both too old to change opinions which are the result of a long life of inquiry and reflection; but on the suggestion of a former letter of yours, that we ought not to die before we have explained ourselves to each other."[4] Explain themselves to each other they did, in what is surely the richest and most memorable correspondence in our political history; but while the old passions of the 1790s and 1800s had subsided, their renewed friendship did not mean the end of disagreement between them. On the contrary, their correspondence in their reflective retirement years reveals a range and depth of philosophical differences heavy with meaning for their views on slavery—and for American liberalism. To make this clear, we must recall their old controversies.

During their political conflicts of the 1790s, Jefferson celebrated liberty and equality and, as an ardent believer in progress, scorned the dead hand of the past. A tribune for all those who insisted on political democracy, a champion of the common man, he welcomed the French Revolution as a herald of the new age. Preaching this new creed, he led the revolution of 1800, becoming, after his presidency, a symbol of liberty.[5] By contrast, his predecessor, Adams, insisted on the conservative values of hierarchy and self-discipline, respect for authority, reverence for his ancestors, and institutional constraints on popular passions. He recoiled in horror from the Revolution in France and became a leading Federalist.[6] Encumbered by his elitist and therefore "irrelevant" version of republicanism, however, and embittered by his defeat in 1800, he left the White House for a relatively obscure retirement.[7] His party would never win another national election. "Adams was a voice from the past," writes Merrill Peterson, "while Jefferson continued to voice the aspirations . . . of American democracy."[8] Peterson's judgment is accurate enough on most issues, though it overlooks the important areas of agreement suggested by their collaboration during the 1770s and 1780s. In the case of slavery, however, his claim is simply mistaken. It was Jefferson who clung to the past and Adams who showed the way to the future.

Toward the end of his life, the ordinarily optimistic Jefferson became apprehensive about the drift of American politics, in particular the North's growing opposition to chattel slavery.[9] Although he was a strong opponent of slavery early in his career, in later years his public opposition ceased. As president, he refused to discuss slavery at all, and by 1820, agitated by the Missouri controversy, he called for slavery's spread throughout the Louisiana Purchase. Northern opposition to admitting Missouri as a slave state, Jefferson thought, would promote sectional rancor without helping the slaves. In effect, he believed that Americans could find happiness in areas with slavery as well as in those without it.[10]

Adams shared some of Jefferson's caution. As a political conservative concerned about governmental authority and control,[11] he worried about all demands for universal emancipation, and he feared that suddenly freeing the angry slaves would endanger the whites.[12] Even his disagreements in the 1770s with his wife, Abigail, on such subjects as slavery and the position of women reveal a more fundamental agreement that the despotic dominion by one human being over another is intolerable. By 1829 the same development of the slavery controversy that troubled Jefferson left the usually conservative Adams relatively unperturbed. In his retirement, primarily in his private correspondence (to others than Jefferson), he moved toward his wife's view of slavery. Some of his reasons were prudential, having to do with the effects of slavery on others besides slaves; hence his concern for white workers and distrust of the "aristocratic" slave owners. For such reasons, reversing Jefferson's view of sectional issues, he opposed permitting slavery in Missouri.[13] The prudential shaded into the ethical, however, and a concern for the harm slavery did to white workers was joined by a concern for the slaves themselves: "If the gangrene is not stopped — I can see nothing but Insurrection . . . till at last the Whites will be exasperated to Madness — [and] shall be wicked enough to exterminate the negroes." Thus the Missourians ought to be moved by "feelings of humanity" in deciding "to exclude slavery sternly from their state."[14] For all Adams's concern for white workers, this appeal anticipated later antislavery arguments that were embraced by his son John Quincy and his grandson Charles Francis and would help lead the antislavery struggle.

Here, then, is the slavery anomaly: A deeply conservative side to Jefferson's genuine egalitarianism was matched in 1820 by a potentially radical, prophetic side to Adams's equally genuine suspicions about popular passion. Heavily qualified as their positions on slavery were, the egalitarian Jefferson had become increasingly protective of the institution, and the conservative Adams came to see it as both morally evil and politically dangerous.

This anomaly, however, was not an aberration in which Adams and Jefferson somehow violated all their most important principles. Nor did it simply reflect differences between them, either in personal or regional interests or in racial attitudes. It is true enough that their racial attitudes and economic and political interests were so pronounced that we are tempted to think these explain the positions on slavery they came to adopt. Adams, for example, had little that was disparaging to say about blacks. On the other hand, even the younger Jefferson who openly opposed slavery had asserted in his *Notes on Virginia* that blacks were inferior to whites,[15] and his draft of the Declaration had treated blacks and whites, as well as Americans and the British, as different peoples. Then, too, many of Jefferson's northern followers were racially prejudiced.[16] It might also be argued that their eventual shift on slavery was but the inevitable recognition of where their economic and political interests really lay. Jefferson derived his income, after all, from his extensive plantations that relied on slave labor, and his political career ultimately depended on backing from other southern whites. More broadly, the introduction of the cotton gin confounded the Founders' hopes about slavery's demise by making slave labor an increasingly central feature of the southern economy. In these circumstances, it became steadily more difficult for Jefferson, or any other southern leader, to oppose the institution. By contrast, this argument runs, Adams could so freely invoke the "feelings of humanity" in the Missouri crisis because neither he nor a significant number of his followers had any economic stake in slavery. On the contrary, slavery was also moving toward the center of sectional tensions over such issues as tariffs and internal improvements, and such issues inevitably affected the climate in which Adams and his fellow Yankees thought and talked about slavery.

Nevertheless, the movement in their positions on slavery cannot be seen as merely an expression of their changing interests, comfortable as that explanation may seem. For one thing, neither Jefferson nor Adams, although each man had changed his position on slavery by 1820, seemed to think he had disrupted his intellectual universe. In fact neither man had. It is indeed precisely that intellectual universe, along with triggering economic and social causes, that accounts for, or at any rate *allowed* for, the evolution of their views on the peculiar institution.

Counterintuitive as it may seem, my claim is that these positions on slavery exemplify the basic polarity of the humanist and reformed sides of the American liberal tradition. Each man's shift on slavery was firmly rooted in his most fundamental beliefs, in those categories and commitments—political, social, and overtly philosophic—that shaped his view of politics and all human life.

In coming to terms with slavery in their own ways, the "radical" Virginian focused on the concrete and worldly interests and concerns of particular human beings; the "conservative" Yankee, on the other hand, insisted on the central importance of a divinely given and therefore transcendent moral law. This basic opposition, in turn, involved two further sets of questions of a distinctly ethical and philosophic nature:

1. How important is it as a principle of politics to balance the competing claims, rights, and preferences of different human beings, as opposed simply to doing one's (individual) moral duty? In addressing this question, the two men addressed the issues of happiness, moral obligation, and human freedom.

2. How important ethically are the observable facts of a given
    situation; in particular, what deference should one accord
    the existing social practices and institutions of a free society?
    Here the two men considered both the character of human
    rationality in determining social action and the philosophic
    issues of epistemology and ontology.

In exploring these issues we shall begin with Jefferson.

JEFFERSON'S HUMANIST LIBERALISM

Jefferson's humanist liberalism was firmly grounded in a sensationalist and materialist philosophy, a "creed of materialism," as Jefferson
himself put it, "supported" by John Locke. Amending Descartes, he
wrote Adams that " 'I feel: therefore I exist.' . . . When once we quit
the basis of sensation, all is in the wind." He thus rejected "all or-
gans of information . . . but my senses." The reality thus known was
thoroughly material. "I feel bodies which are not myself: there are
other existences then. I call them *matter.* . . . Where there is an ab-
sence of matter, I call it *void,* or *nothing, immaterial space.* On the
basis of sensation, of matter and motion, we may erect . . . all [our]
. . . certainties."[17] On this philosophical basis, indeed, he erected his
ethics.

Well-regulated personal pleasures and a tranquil private happiness were among Jefferson's preoccupations.[18] He commended the
French for excelling Americans in "the pleasures of the table," and
savored these delights himself.[19] He disliked pain in himself or others. "For what good end," he asked Adams, could "the sensations of
Grief . . . be intended? All our other passions, within proper
bounds, have an useful object . . . [but] what is the use of grief?"[20]
Jefferson coupled this concern with a charitable presumption about
every individual's motives, including his own. In Miller's words, he
believed "in original goodness, not original sin; if man had fallen
from grace it was [only] . . . because he had submitted his own free
will to the oppressive rule of kings, priests, and nobles."[21] In his view,
when "our duties and interests . . . seem to be at variance, we ought
to suspect some fallacy in our reasonings."[22] He was "an Epicurean,"
Peterson adds, "though of sober mien, to whom emotional torment
and self-flagellation were alien." "Never [a diarist] . . . [he] kept re-
cords of everything . . . except the state of his soul."[23]

Nor was this concern exclusively self-regarding.[24] Jefferson followed the Scottish Enlightenment in holding that pleasure came

from helping others as well as from satisfying oneself. "Self-love," Jefferson wrote, "is the sole antagonist of virtue," and he assailed Hobbes's egoism.[25] As he wrote Abigail Adams, "I am never happier than when I am performing good offices for good people. . . ."[26] This regard for others included a relativistic utilitarianism. "Nature," he remarked "has constituted *utility* to man, [as] the standard and test of virtue. Men living . . . under different circumstances . . . may have different utilities; the same act, therefore, may be useful, and consequently virtuous in one country—[even though it] is injurious and vicious in another differently circumstanced."[27]

But what if people in the same society have conflicting goals? Like Locke, Jefferson thought in terms of rights. As a good humanist, he thought there was little if any room for an obligation to obey God or some transcendent moral law. Instead, individuals had the right to define their own happiness and then pursue it. Because every individual's rights must be weighted equally, no person or group deserved special consideration. Accordingly, he was deeply ambivalent about demands for his continued public service. As he wrote to his protege James Monroe, "If we are made in some degree for others, yet, in a greater, we are made for ourselves . . . [A situation in which] a man had less rights in himself than . . . his neighbors [have in directing his activities] . . . would be slavery."[28] Thus the controlling principle was one of balance—here the balance between Jefferson's own right to happiness, as he defined it for himself, and the claims of his fellow citizens.

Jefferson had a parallel understanding of human freedom. If individuals define happiness for themselves, then they should be as free and unobstructed as possible in pursuing their self-determined goals. As Cooke remarks, Jefferson's position "was . . . very much in the tradition of what . . . Berlin has called 'negative freedom,'" or exemption from the coercion of others.[29] This stand, in turn, reinforced Jefferson's fundamental commitment to fairness in weighing competing moral claims. If freedom means unobstructed action, and if individuals and groups have conflicting goals, an equitable arrangement will probably subject everyone to some restraint. In his own words, freedom is rightful only "within the limits drawn around us by the equal rights of others."[30]

This commitment to establishing an ethical balance also supported Jefferson's emphasis on the moral relevance of the factual, of the observable realities of the world around him. The crucial connection here is between the idea of negative freedom and an instrumental view of rationality. Individuals have the right to choose their own goals without asking permission of others. Others can observe such choices, but there is no reasonable basis on which to criticize them. Thus an individual's action is rational to the extent that it is an effective way to secure whatever goal the actor happens to have. This point illuminates Jefferson's noted enthusiasm for collecting facts. Assuming that an individual's chosen goal will not unduly interfere with the rights of others, the only questions that can be asked legitimately by outsiders are empirical rather than evaluative: Are the actions that an individual undertakes the most effective available? Jefferson himself devoted considerable attention to this question of practical efficacy. It shaped his view of education, of travel, and the way he ran his plantation. "The study of the law," he wrote a nephew, "qualifies a man to be useful to himself, to his neighbors, and to the public." Fortunately, it is also "the most certain stepping-stone to [political] preferment."[31]

This orientation is broadly consistent with Jefferson's humanism. One of the Enlightenment's deepest impulses was its revolt against everything supernatural and mysterious in medieval and feudal culture in favor of the natural, the human, the commonplace — and the observable.

JEFFERSON'S PARADOXICAL DISPOSITIONS

No claim can be sustained that Jefferson's humanist liberalism *directly* caused his proslavery shift. Methodologically, the difficulty is that stable beliefs cannot cause changes in attitude or behavior. Substantively, the problem is that slavery violated Jefferson's general liberal commitment to political freedom and equality, as well as his more specific beliefs in altruism and egalitarianism. So too, his humanist celebration of the solid, observable, and therefore familiar would seem to run against the unwarranted pretensions of any social elite. French aristocrats or southern slave holders might wear expensive clothes and have refined tastes, but for a materialist like Jefferson, all human beings clearly belonged to one biological species — and by virtue of that fact, they enjoyed the same natural rights. These beliefs supported his attack on the French Old Regime and on Hamilton's social and economic vision; the latter not only because it favored those who were already rich but also because it seemed likely to produce new, governmentally created social and economic inequalities.

From this perspective, the youthful Jefferson's opposition to slavery would seem to be a matter of course. In any event, many of the European philosophes whom Jefferson admired joined a society called Amis des Noirs precisely because they moved from their humanist premises to antislavery conclusions. Thus Jefferson's humanism would seem to constitute an ethical disposition to support human equality and oppose human slavery.

Just how, then, did this humanist liberalism dispose either Jefferson himself or his northern followers to protect slavery? As he wrote in the Declaration, these beliefs included, first, human equality at least with respect to basic political rights; second, the ordering of these rights in terms of life, liberty, and the pursuit of happiness; third, instituting government with the consent of the governed. How could those beliefs ever condone slavery? Again, tolerance was a centerpiece of Jefferson's political creed: He detested every governmentally sponsored religious or cultural orthodoxy. How, then, could tolerance come to apply to chattel slavery?

Jefferson offers a clue in his draft of the Declaration. There he berated the English king, not just for imposing slavery on the colonists but for then threatening white lives by trying to incite the slaves to revolt. Evil though slavery was in the abstract, the issue became much more complex once the institution was in place—and presumably enjoyed substantial popular support. This stand can be connected to the Declaration's more fundamental principles. Leaving aside for the moment any possible conflict between the rights of the two races, there is also a tension between the very ideas of individual rights and consenting to the governance of a body of citizens.

For Jefferson, the doctrine of consent, supplemented by his devotion to maximizing human unity, had two important consequences. First, a regime based on consent was intrinsically worthy of support. Second, the regime could only fulfill its obligations through an inherently political process, one that was devoted to helping all its citizens pursue their own self-defined happiness. Accordingly, each decision had to satisfy as many citizens as possible, and the process had to preserve the regime itself so that it could continue to meet its obligations. One could not simply say, as in a Lockean state of nature, that the rights of every individual must be respected. On occasion, citizens might have to sacrifice their own claims either to preserve the regime itself or to help it fulfill its obligations. In this way, Jefferson's doctrine of consent inspired both loyalty to liberal political regimes and support for the process of compromise and accommodation—that is, balancing conflicting claims—characteristic of genuinely democratic politics.

This spirit marked not only the celebrated compromises of the Constitutional Convention but also many key episodes of Jefferson's political career: his reluctant agreement to the assumption of state debts in exchange for locating the new capital city on the Potomac; his middle position on the notorious Yazoo land frauds; his pragmatic decision to buy Louisiana, contrary to his own strict Constitutional principles; his eventual openness to manufacturing as a response to British threats; and above all, his skillful management of the Republican party.[32] In every case, his pursuit of his own preferences was affected by both his assessment of the balance of political forces and the overriding need to preserve the new republic. When Jefferson would not compromise, as in his support for the Revolution and religious freedom and in his opposition to the Alien and Sedition Acts, the issue involved governmental threats to individual freedom. Otherwise, he was typically devoted to harmonizing interests through compromise and accommodation.

Further, as Jefferson pointed out to the defeated and anxious Federalists in his First Inaugural, "though the will of the majority must in all cases prevail, that will, to be rightful, must be reasonable." He then went on to assure them that "the minority possess their equal rights, which . . . to violate would be oppression." He suggested in that address that a genuinely free process of argument and debate would eventually lead to the right political decision.[33] He also accepted the argument of Adam Smith and others that economic activity would be most generally beneficial if only the relevant markets were genuinely free. In each case, the right setting—a republican government or a free market—would produce good results. Here, it seems, was a presumption in favor of those social practices and institutions that had emerged and flourished in a liberal regime, and here, too, was a further warrant for accommodation. As a familiar maxim of democratic politics puts it, in order to get along, one has to go along with established institutions as well as influential politicians. This spirit of accommodation and free interchange would prove as relevant, later, to the interests of slavery as to the worried Federalists of 1801.

Two features of Jefferson's political outlook could be used to argue against a strong antislavery stand. First, with respect to consent and opinion, slavery was strongly supported by many whites in the South and at least tolerated by many others in the North. The idea of compromise suggested taking these views seriously. Second, with respect to social experience, slavery was an important social and economic institution that had in fact flourished in America's liberal society. At the least, therefore, it had to be treated circumspectly. On both counts, then, there was a political disposition to protect the institution.

To this point, the paradox remains unresolved. Jefferson's humanist ethics seemed to dispose him in one way; his humanist politics seemed to dispose him in another. Early in his career, the balance between them had an antislavery tilt. The question, then, is what triggering conditions caused him to shift to a protective attitude — and why did these conditions have the effect they did? Several events come readily to mind. First, a series of slave revolts, most notably in Santo Domingo and then in the United States, heightened white fears for their safety and even survival.[34] Second, the introduction of the cotton gin made slavery a much more important, and seemingly permanent, feature of southern life in particular and the American economy in general. Partially as a result, southern opinion (on which much of Jefferson's political influence depended) increasingly turned against any antislavery agitation. Finally, the great American experiment in republican government, to which Jefferson had devoted his whole career, seemed more and more secure, more and more successful. Thus, an attack on any of the regime's important political or social institutions, including slavery, seemed more problematic. Taken together, these developments reinforced just those elements in Jefferson's thought that argued for protecting slavery as an existing institution.

In its own terms, I believe this argument is convincing. One question remains: How could Jefferson make this move with so little sense that he was contradicting any of his basic beliefs? To answer that question, we must examine the specifically humanist way in which his creed understood such liberal tenets as freedom, rationality, and human well-being.

SLAVERY AND HUMANIST LIBERALISM

Point by point, Jefferson's basic humanist values reinforced his political disposition to protect slavery. To be sure, his commitment to negative freedom, to the norm of unobstructed action, would seem to favor the slaves' emancipation, since it would surely increase their liberty. But as we have seen, when the people have conflicting preferences, protecting or increasing the freedom of some necessarily limits that of others. As a practical matter, every viable liberal regime will constrain everyone to some extent. In particular, abolition would just as surely limit the freedom — the unobstructed action — of those who favored slavery or owned slaves. True to his altruistic and charitable attitudes, toward himself as well as others, Jefferson never seems seriously to have reproached himself for owning slaves.

More generally, Jefferson's principles required him to recognize the fears of southern whites about the reprisals they would suffer if their slaves were ever freed. Here was a compelling interest to be balanced against the slaves' claims to freedom. As Jefferson himself put it, first in the Declaration and then forty-four years later, the blacks' right to freedom conflicted with the whites' ultimately more important right to life. Nor did he entirely ignore the white masters' property rights.[35] As early as 1781, he could refer rather matter of factly to the southerners' "lands, slaves, and other property."[36] Once again, it was necessary to weigh competing objectives.

At the same time, the relativistic side of Jefferson's utilitarianism sharply qualified the blanket condemnation of any institution. The key question was always the institution's effect in particular cases. As immoral as slavery might be in general, the institution had flourished in a free society, and its persistence could be persuasively justified in the South where racial conflict was a real threat. Specifically, Jefferson qualified his universalism with a certain particularism. If the two races were separate peoples, as Jefferson suggested in his draft of the Declaration, the two races had not contracted with each other to observe and mutually enforce their several natural rights. For that reason, those blacks who were freed might well be expected to be particularly vengeful. For even conscientious whites, then, the primary obligation was presumably to other members of their own political community.

Jefferson's empirical orientation, his philosophic sensationalism and materialism, and his respect for observable facts and the institutions of a free society proved comforting to southern whites in other ways. His humanist belief in progress, for example, meant that historical facts could determine values. Given the political freedom to pursue individually defined goals, social arrangements that survive and flourish can be presumed to be progressive and therefore valuable. As an integral part of American society, slavery could readily be seen to fit this description.

Again, Jefferson surely believed in human equality in the abstract, but his empiricist outlook made it difficult to treat this belief as a postulate from which one might begin to reason. Even if assertions about human equality might all be true, they still had to be verified by sense perception and more specifically by an empirical inquiry, e.g., into the differences between the two races.[37] Whatever the causes that kept the slaves from acquiring literacy or other valuable skills, the observable fact, as he saw it, was their intellectual inferiority to whites. Jefferson's empiricism, of course, did not *require* him to read the facts this way; he could have identified the blacks' problems as a consequence of their bondage. Given his self-interest, racial fears, and loyalty to his region, Jefferson's empiricism made it *easier* for him to reach his conclusion.

A similar account applies to Jefferson's materialism. In fact, his notorious discussion in the *Notes on Virginia* (Query 14) emphasizes those racial differences that were physical and therefore readily observable.[38] What is more, this outlook encouraged the view that these observed patterns of racial difference and inequality would persist. If human beings are essentially material entities, their future development is likely to be consistent with their physical makeup, including the physiological and thus observable differences between the races.

None of these considerations refutes the claim that Jefferson was committed to the liberal values of freedom, equality, and individual rights. Jefferson's devotion to compromise and accommodation did not block his early opposition to slavery nor his general support for trying to help the common people on most economic issues. Problems arose only when political controversy touched on an institution that was deeply embedded in a society's fabric and was therefore entitled to respect from Jefferson's empiricist outlook. He voiced one version of this attitude when he suggested that the utility of an institution or practice would differ from one situation to another. He applied it in practice when he urged his French friends to take the existing situation into account and therefore to move cautiously in reforming the Old Regime.[39] It was particularly relevant to his own society and polity. First, Jefferson was a good democrat who had a profound confidence in the good sense of the common people; his humanist philosophy helped extend that optimism to those institutions and practices that had developed in a free society. In other words, the fact that the American polity and society was liberal in *general* created a presumption in favor of any *particular* social institution that had flourished within its confines. In any case, Jefferson had less and less to say, over time, at least in public, on slavery's evil character. Second, slavery had deeply embedded itself in American life. Thus any attempt to uproot it would threaten the health, or indeed survival, of the liberal republic to which Jefferson had devoted his life. Here, then, was the real importance of Jefferson's humanist liberalism. His most basic beliefs rationalized and legitimated a process by which his political disposition to protect slavery eventually overrode his ethical disposition to attack it.

ADAMS'S REFORMED LIBERALISM

Like Jefferson, Adams valued balance and political compromise. His theory of republicanism focused on the appropriate balance among both political institutions and social groups. At the end of his administration, he frustrated the belligerent Hamiltonians in his own cabinet by deciding to avoid a bitterly controversial war with France. Nevertheless, he was no humanist liberal.

As Peterson puts it, Adams "was a zealot, not about any particular creed, but about religion. It was in his blood and [it] had weighed on his mind all of his life."[40] Without religion, he thought, there could be no philosophy,[41] and he repeatedly praised his Puritan forebears for their morals, courage, intellectuality, and even their anti-Catholicism.[42] He also embraced much of their traditional piety. For all his disagreements with orthodox Calvinists on many issues, he shared their belief in human inferiority and ignorance when compared to God's infinite and inscrutable majesty. There "never was but one being who can Understand the Universe," he wrote Jefferson in 1813. "And . . . it is not only vain but wicked for insects to pretend to comprehend it." Because "the World is . . . a Riddle and an Enigma,"[43] he thought humility was the only appropriate response. The human soul "ought to fill itself with a meek and humble anxiety."[44] Here, to be sure, was an almost Kantian focus on the limits of the human mind, anticipating the Transcendentalism of the next generation.

However, Adams also insisted on the individual's responsibility to act in the light of transcendent moral standards, rather than be guided by Jefferson's sensationalist and materialist pursuit of a self-defined happiness. Indeed he *defined* that state, happiness, as had Aristotle, holding that it "consists in virtue,"[45] not in a subjective sense of well-being. He was therefore deeply suspicious of pleasure as a goal in human life, at one point proclaiming his own devotion to "business alone."[46] As he wrote in his diary in 1756, "He is not a wise man . . . that has left one Passion in his Soul unsubdued." John Adams was no hedonist.[47]

Adams could not accept Jefferson's view of human freedom. He agreed, to be sure, on the importance of negative freedom, particularly the right of conscience, and on the need to restrict the negative liberty of some in order to protect that of others. "I have a right," he wrote, "to resist him [who] shall take it into his head . . . that he has a right to take my property without my consent."[48] But liberty for Adams also had a positive side. One can undertake an activity only if one has the ability to perform it. Thus freedom *from* the "Passions," he believed, meant freedom *to* cultivate one's faculties, physical, intellectual, and moral. For his Puritan forebears the object was to secure the greater glory of God. For the more secular Adams, the object was to develop one's talents and abilities to become more useful to oneself and others. In a sense, liberty defined and empowered the responsible human being and indeed *enabled* the citizen to do his duty. "Liberty, according to my metaphysics," he wrote, "is an intellectual quality . . . it is a self-determining power in an intellectual agent. It implies thought and choice and power."[49] A central goal, then, was to foster general self-improvement, including the improvement of his and other people's moral faculties.

The contrast with Jefferson is clear. Given his belief in negative liberty and tranquillity, the Virginian placed less emphasis on fundamental changes in individuals. Education and experience would help in pursuing one's goals more effectively, but even without such assistance, all normal individuals could be trusted to identify their goals, i.e., to define happiness for themselves — and then act altruistically where appropriate. For Adams, however, positive liberty meant that completely free individuals would develop themselves by systematically cultivating their faculties.

As a result, he put relatively little emphasis on balancing competing claims. The true moral imperative was to make sure that individuals did their duty and obeyed an appropriate moral law. Public service offers an interesting case in point. Where Jefferson sometimes regarded it as a burden imposed on him by others for their benefit, Adams saw it as an opportunity for conscientious individuals to undertake self-improvement. The obligation of the rulers, he wrote John Taylor, is "to exert all their intellectual liberty to employ all their faculties, talents, and power for the public, general universal good . . . [and] not for their own separate good or the interest of any party."[50] Because public service offered this opportunity, the issue of balancing the public's interest with that of the individual official became irrelevant.

This stand was broadly reinforced by Adams's epistemology and ontology. In an 1816 letter, Adams dismissed Jefferson's materialism as inconsistent with human liberty, conscience, and morality.[51] At other times, he resorted to skepticism. The "question of spirit and matter" he wrote Jefferson in 1820, was "nugatory because we have neither evidence nor idea of either."[52] Nor could sensory experience resolve matters. Against Jefferson's sensationalism, he held that the "essences of body and mind" cannot be penetrated by "our senses or instruments." "Incision, knives and microscopes make no discoveries in this region."[53] What is more, the mind also provided a knowledge independent of sensory experience.[54] "Philosophy which is the result of Reason," he wrote Jefferson, "is the first, the original Revelation of the Creator to his Creature, Man."[55] In effect, then, Adams rejected any effort such as Jefferson's to ground notions of human well-being in the sensory experience of the human animal. There was, instead, "a law of right reason common to God and man" that is essential for "all human reasoning on the moral government of the universe."[56]

ADAMS'S COMPLEX DISPOSITIONS
ON SLAVERY

Just as Jefferson's humanist liberalism sustained two seemingly opposed dispositions with regard to slavery, Adams's reformed outlook pointed in two quite different directions. His belief in social and individual development upheld many of his political stands against the Jeffersonians. Despite his reservations about banks, he loyally supported Hamilton's economic program because he believed in the government's obligation to promote individual and collective improvement. Here was the Federalists', and later the Whigs', commitment to government activism that the Jeffersonians assailed as conservative or paternalistic.

This stress on the cultivation of human faculties also implied that levels of development would almost certainly vary from one individual to another. For Adams, these personal differences posed a double threat to republican regimes that required a plainly conservative response. On one side, the able and ambitious might well use their abilities to dominate the government for their own benefit. On the other, the uneducated and undisciplined common people might succumb to demagoguery and become unruly mobs, as they did in the French Revolution and Shays's Rebellion. He prescribed the same familiar solution for both problems: a system of checks and balances in which each governmental institution represents a different social stratum, with the people dominating the lower house of the legislature and the elite "ostracized," as he put it, in the upper chamber. Although Adams angrily denied that his stand favored aristocratic government, it did rely on the well-educated and socially successful to control popular passions.

This generally conservative outlook did not ensure a protective stand on slavery. Other northern Federalists often charged their egalitarian opponents, including Jefferson, with quietly but hypocritically condoning slavery.[57] For our purposes, the important point is that Adams's own doctrine of piety had a similar thrust. If every individual was vastly inferior to God, then all forms of human pride and selfishness were surely unwarranted. From that position it was but a short step to the conclusion, which Abigail had implied in her 1776 letter to him, that slavery is unGodly—impious—because it elevates some human beings to a position over others, an elevation that belonged to God alone. Also, Adams's devotion to a republican system of checks and balances was meant to prevent anyone, be it English rioters or French or American radicals, from exercising absolute power.[58] Excessive power, and the pride that went with it, often tempted the powerful to act on desires that were contrary to their self-development or that of others. As Abigail argued in her letter of 1776, a concern of this sort could readily acquire an antislavery cast.[59]

Adams's position on slavery thus exhibited a tension between development and restraint. On one side, he was deeply worried about restraining the passions of the untutored. On the other, if self-development was so important for the species, then the slaves ought to be allowed to cultivate their faculties—and they presumably could not do so if they were owned as chattel. Here, then, are two central questions: First, if there were both pro and antislavery elements in Adams's outlook, how can we say that his position, as a whole, was disposed against the institution? Second, given Adams's obvious conservatism, what triggering conditions brought that antislavery disposition into play—what changes in American society or culture actually produced an antislavery shift by Adams himself, and to a greater degree, the Adams family?

Knowing as we do the eventual antislavery drift of the Adams family, it is not hard to identify changes that resolved the tension in his outlook. Consider first the perception that the American republican experiment seemed increasingly secure because it was a proven success. Given that security, there was less need for restraint, because popular protests could be seen to pose a less serious threat to

the political order. Accordingly, there was more room to tolerate antislavery agitation and less need to worry about its consequences. At
the same time, of course, the cotton gin had made slavery a much
more important, and seemingly permanent, feature of the American economy. If slavery subjected one human being to the illicit
domination of another, its growing importance could become a reason for opposing and not for protecting it: The individual slaves
faced permanent subjection to their masters, and the number of
slaves so dominated was likely to increase.

Although these two factors, taken together, may have helped shift
the balance between development and restraint that produced
Adams's ambivalence, by themselves they seem insufficient to have
shaken Adams's deeply conservative outlook. As it happened, however, there was a third triggering condition that had a major impact
on Adams's outlook, namely the emergence of a much less elitist and
less deterministic current within New England's Calvinist tradition.

According to the orthodox Calvinist doctrines of predestination
and original sin, most individuals were doomed to damnation by a
divine decree. Only a few redeemed saints would help shape the
world according to God's plan—and to better perform this task they
would systematically develop their faculties. These beliefs made it
feasible—though certainly not necessary—to defend slavery as a re-
grettable but useful restraint on willful sinners. Indeed, this stand
paralleled one for which Adams had some sympathy: keeping the
slaves under control of masters whose intellectual faculties were
much better developed.

This orthodox argument for protecting slavery became increasingly difficult to assert once the elitist and deterministic doctrine of
predestination was abandoned. According to the new view, all individuals were eligible for salvation and could achieve it by following
the way of the saint through the exercise of their own free will. Following that path meant showing devotion to God by cultivating one's
moral, intellectual and physical faculties in order the better to serve
the divine cause, and it was just such a path that the slave masters
prevented their chattel from following. In this regard, slavery egre-
giously violated the obligations that human beings owed their Creator, not just each other. Not surprisingly, the Second Great Awakening of the early 1800s, which powerfully advanced this new liberal
creed, also spawned the abolitionist agitation of the 1830s.

The resemblance between Adams's own religion and the Awakening was only approximate. Where the Awakening was enthusiastic
and trinitarian, Adams was a philosophically attuned Unitarian.

Where the Awakening stimulated the abolitionist movement, Adams's children and grandchildren became Whigs and Republicans. But if the Adams family did not experience a direct link between evangelical Christianity and abolition, their politics did undergo a somewhat parallel development. Specifically, Adams's son, John Quincy, responded much more than his father to the democratic currents that helped produce both the Jacksonian revolution in American politics and the Second Great Awakening in American Protestantism. Over time, the son therefore incorporated the ideas of political equality and unconstrained self-development into his political rhetoric. At one level, then, the liberal religious beliefs that the two men shared had more direct influence on the political views of the son than on the father's.[60] But toward the end of his life, John Adams himself began to look to his son for political guidance.

In retrospect, at least, these changes do account for Adams's shift on slavery. Still, as with Jefferson we must ask how he accomplished his shift with no real sense of contradicting his basic values. To answer this question, we must ask what features of Adams's reformed liberalism encouraged the emergence of a moderate though still fervently moral antislavery ethos. As I shall now show, the elements of Adams's thought that he largely shared with his New England forebears and that separated him from Jefferson made it especially and increasingly difficult for the Adams family to remain indifferent to human slavery.

SLAVERY AND REFORMED LIBERALISM

Once again, a comparison is helpful. The young Jefferson saw slavery as a moral evil and wished for its elimination when practicable, but this desire had to be balanced against competing considerations of both utility and rights. Adams, in rejecting a subjective, self-determined happiness as an ultimate moral guide, undercut the whole rationale for this concern. Consider, once again, the issue of public service. For Adams this activity offered an opportunity both to cultivate one's own faculties and to serve others. Consequently, the positive freedom of all would benefit. More generally, because there was no necessary conflict between developing one's own faculties and those of other people, there was no presumption that one group's freedom or well-being would necessarily conflict with those of another. Indeed, the public servant had a clear obligation to help others follow the right path. Like his Puritan forebears, therefore, Adams favored educating the slaves, however much this position became anathema in the South after his death.[61]

This analysis applied to policies and institutions as well as to the actions of individuals. Some institutions and policies might help both oneself and others develop their faculties; other institutions or policies might be generally harmful, regardless of the preferences involved. Here too, the question of weighing valid but competing claims could not arise, for either the abolitionists or the Adams family. As Adams himself suggested in his comments about the Missouri Crisis, the institution blighted the moral development of the slave owners as much as it prevented the intellectual development of the slaves. On this view, everyone would benefit from emancipation.

As we have seen, Jefferson's shift on slavery also rested on his empiricist regard for what he took to be facts, notably that blacks were inferior and that slavery had a growing importance in American life. Here too, though, Adams's basic beliefs led down a different path because he refused to take individual goals as automatically deserving respect. Instead, he submitted all such goals to moral evaluation and objected to any group's having unlimited power to pursue whatever aims it wished, be it husbands, wives, or the British authorities. For Abigail in 1776, this list included slave holders, as it did for John (at least on the Missouri question) in 1820. Later, their children and grandchildren would make open war against the slave power.

The deeper contrast with Jefferson was more explicitly philosophical. Consistent with his ontology and epistemology, Jefferson stressed racial differences that were mainly physical and empirically observable. Adams rejected this philosophy because he believed the decisive issue was the condition of an individual's soul, that is, an immaterial object that cannot be directly observed. On Adams's view, then, Jefferson was not simply wrong about the facts. The more fundamental mistake was to rely in the first place on irrelevant empirical observations about racial differences. Instead, Adams asserted the moral equality of human beings, i.e., the equality of souls, as a postulate from which one should begin to reason — rather than the conclusion of an empirical, scientific inquiry. For him, this belief warranted supporting education for all, black and white alike. For his family, this same dignity required emancipation.

By rejecting Jefferson's concern with balance and facts, Adams's reformed liberalism made every feature of his society open to moral criticism, no matter how popular or well established. For this reason, the changes considered here, i.e., the success of the American republican experiment, slavery's apparent permanence, and the spread of a more liberal Calvinism, can be seen to have encouraged antislavery attitudes. The Civil War did not come in 1861 simply because there were differences of opinion about the morality of slavery: It came, in part at least, because some antislavery northerners undertook a sustained emotional crusade that eventually enlisted relative moderates such as John Quincy and Charles Francis Adams. Crusades require crusaders, those committed enough to sacrifice for a cause, and here the least humanist feature of Adams's reformed liberalism, the Calvinist tradition of piety, was crucial.

A perceived contrast between an almost worthless humanity and a remote and finally inscrutable God may not seem a likely source for a moral crusade. If God were so remote that divine will and intention were beyond human knowledge — if the human world were dead in sin, or at least profoundly removed from a majestic, perfect God — how could a conscientious believer confidently adopt any militant cause? Again, if all humankind were so deficient, how could any one of them presume to launch a moral crusade against established social institutions and practices? The short answer is that the great distance between a majestic God and most human beings made it all the more vital to be among those who were singled out for redemption. If that redemption was associated with actively serving God, then the consequence may be militant activism, rather than quiescence. In other words, the very sinfulness of the human state made it especially imperative that the redeemed believers distinguish themselves by actively seeking to remake the world. To be sure, the world was so morally ambiguous that the right path was never fully knowable, human efforts never perfectly successful, and every achievement only provisional. But it followed that every step forward left many more to be taken, and the efforts of the righteous had to be especially intense and unremitting. This profound tension between the human and the divine could be best relieved by throwing oneself into the activity and drama of a moral, reformative crusade — be it the Puritan Revolution, the Great Migration to colonial New England, or Yankee Calvinist support for the American Revolution.

Skeptical as he was about political enthusiasms, Adams recognized just this connection between piety and moral duty. "The faculties of our understanding," he wrote Jefferson in 1825, "are not adequate to penetrate the Universe." After thus expressing his piety, he moved immediately to the issue of moral conduct. "Let us do our duty which is, to do as we would be done by . . . ."[62] In the right circumstances—those of his children and grandchildren after 1830—this sentiment could be more than a demand for good conduct in one's usual calling. It could sustain a prophetic call for a relentless moral struggle.

LIBERAL MORAL CODE
VERSUS LIBERAL CONTEXT

Adam's reformed liberalism in and of itself was not directed against any single type of institution, policy, or practice. It sustained his distaste for the Revolution in France in the 1780s and his opposition to Jefferson's egalitarian politics after 1790 as easily as it supported his own revolutionary stand in the 1770s. The point, instead, is that approval for any such institution or social arrangement was always provisional. No matter how socially important an institution had become, or how much it conformed to the preferences of a political faction, the decisive issue was always one's ethical obligations in respect to it. Institutions repugnant to the moral law must be condemned. As reformed liberalism came to assert the dignity and moral equality of every human soul, this stand turned against slavery.

Here the difference between Jefferson and Adams was one of context vs. moral code. For Jefferson, the essential point about American politics was the liberal character of the context, of the regime and society, in which politics took place. Institutions and practices deserved support because the context from which they emerged was so thoroughly liberal, that is, because they allowed individual freedom and required that the expressed preferences of one's compatriots be taken into account. Jefferson's belief in the intrinsic goodness of individuals prompted in him a suspicion of political institutions; eventually, however, his optimism came to include the political and social institutions as well as individuals that flourished in a liberal society. Genuine as his liberal commitments were, they could not readily be used to criticize the central features of either that society or its polity.

Adams shared Jefferson's devotion to these liberal values, but he understood them differently. For the Yankee moralist, they helped constitute a set of norms, an ethical code, not just for regulating interactions among individuals, but for evaluating and criticizing one's social and political world. In particular, he retained the Calvinists' lively sense of human sin, or at least frailty. In that sense, his reformed liberalism drew on enduring features of New England culture that encouraged passing negative moral judgments on the social order. Because he had a much more benign view of the human being than the orthodox Calvinists, he was sometimes inclined to relocate that sin in institutions and social conditions, i.e., intemperance and ignorance. As that tendency became more pronounced in the next generation, it sustained a negative disposition toward human slavery.

Adams, then, helped lay a foundation for a prophetic politics that he did not, and perhaps could not, fully embrace. Others — in his family, his region, and his cultural tradition, including western Whigs like Abraham Lincoln — could and did build on that foundation; but they would add to these enduring features of New England culture — that is, to Adams's neoCalvinist sense of sin and moral obligation — a view of human beings still more egalitarian and voluntarist than Adams's own. Thus they went beyond his view of slavery as an unfortunate practice to see it as profoundly offensive to God or to their own basic moral commitments. As the nation moved closer and closer to secession and civil war, this quarrel with the humanist liberalism became the dominant cleavage in northern politics. What may be less clear — but just as true — is that this same cleavage would continue in later generations and even in our own time.

UNITY, DIVERSITY, AND CIVIC
AMBIVALENCE IN AMERICAN CULTURE

This last claim is too broad to be taken up here, but I do want to suggest that we can find in the tension between Jefferson's humanist and Adams's reformed liberalisms a latent theory of *e pluribus unum*. This theory, I contend, is better able than the standard theory of the liberal community to explain and appraise our national political life. To bring up to date Jefferson's observation in his First Inaugural Address, we are all humanist liberals — we are all reformed liberals. Some of us are more one than the other, no doubt, and it is also surely possible to find something like pure types; without question there are individuals or groups who represent an outlook seemingly wholly committed to one or the other poles of our liberalism. However, I would argue that both liberalisms are necessary to a vibrant American democracy, and that neither, untempered, unmoderated by the other, is sufficient.[63] At the same time, to be self-consciously an American, to embrace both forms of our liberalism, is inescapably to live with ambivalence as we ponder our problematic and ambiguous roles as citizens.

Indeed, for either humanist or reformed liberalism to dominate our politics or our culture would arguably be disastrous for the viability of social diversity and for the integrity and coherence of the nation itself. That this is so is strongly suggested by our history.

Return for a moment to the conflict between the reformed and humanist liberalisms of the antebellum era. For many reformed liberals, the prophetic attack on slavery as un-American and un-Christian was a thinly disguised call for moral homogeneity, that is, for the slave holders to adopt a new moral code. Not surprisingly, perhaps, this attitude led some Yankees, though not the Adams family, into a nativist attack on Roman Catholicism as a foreign, immoral, and undemocratic creed. There was, indeed, a significant, though far from perfect, correlation between opposition to slavery and an anti-Catholic nativism. As we perhaps know more vividly from the experience of such dogmatisms in our own century, the reformed liberalism of John Adams *can*, when it loses its head, descend from the lofty heights of a transcendent moral law to the depths of a rigid and mindless conformity.

On the other hand, the northern humanists who admired Jefferson espoused the sovereignty of individual preferences and thus a right to adopt whatever beliefs or folkways one finds appealing, although they scorned religious or ethnic prejudices. Attractive as this generous and tolerant pluralism can be, especially as we witness the efforts of blacks, ethnic minorities, women, and gays to achieve equal justice in our society, Jefferson's humanist liberalism *can* degenerate into little more than a crass defense of established privilege. For all its professions of respect for individuality and diversity, Jefferson's liberalism in fact capitulated to darkness in the name of balance and accommodation. It lost its heart if not its soul in the face of what must be regarded as the most monstrous evil in all our political history.

As Hannah Arendt once said of behaviorism in the social sciences, the problem with the standard theory of the liberal community is not that it is true, but that it may become true. It is in fact Jefferson's humanist liberalism that serves as a barrier against the monolithic consensus perceived by that theory, and through its concern with compromise and accommodation insists that our unity be a genuine *political* unity. And it is Adams's reformed liberalism that keeps Jefferson's relativism and concern with private satisfactions from degenerating into mere individual and group selfishness. It continues to demand a shared moral vision that in some loose but vital way binds us all together.

NOTES

1. Alexis de Tocqueville, *Democracy in America*, trans. Henry Reeve, rev. Francis Bowen, ed. Phillips Bradley (New York: Vintage Books, 1945); Louis Hartz, *The Liberal Tradition in America* (New York: Harcourt, Brace, 1955); Richard Hofstadter, *The American Political Tradition* (New York: Vintage Books, 1948); Sacvan Bercovitch, *The American Jeremiad* (Madison: University of Wisconsin Press, 1978).

2. J. David Greenstone, "Political Culture and American Political Development: Liberty, Union, and the Liberal Bipolarity," in Karen Orren and Stephen Skowronek, eds., *Studies in American Political Development*, vol. 1 (New Haven, Conn.: Yale University Press, 1986). See also J. David Greenstone, "Against Simplicity: The Cultural Dimensions of the Constitution," *University of Chicago Law Review* 55 (June 1988): 428-49.

3. Franklin I. Gamwell, *Beyond Preference: Liberal Theories of Independent Associations* (Chicago: University of Chicago Press, 1984), p. 9.

4. Jefferson to Adams, 28 October 1813, in Lester J. Cappon, ed., *The Adams-Jefferson Letters: The Complete Correspondence between Thomas Jefferson and Abigail and John Adams* (hereafter cited as "Cappon") (Chapel Hill: University of North Carolina Press, 1959), p. 391.

5. Merrill D. Peterson, *Adams and Jefferson: A Revolutionary Dialogue* (Athens: University of Georgia Press, 1976), pp. 128-29.

6. Daniel Walker Howe, *The Political Culture of the American Whigs* (Chicago: University of Chicago Press, 1979), p. 172; Joyce Appleby, "The New Republican Synthesis and the Changing Political Ideas of John Adams," *American Quarterly* 25, 5 (1973): 591.

7. Gordon S. Wood, *The Creation of the American Republic, 1776-1787* (New York: W. W. Norton, 1969), pp. 574ff., especially 588-89.

8. Peterson, *Adams and Jefferson*, p. 115.

9. Ibid., pp. 125-26.

10. John C. Miller, *The Wolf by the Ears* (New York: Free Press, 1977), pp. 120, 125, 130, 225, 229, and 276-77; Jefferson to Adams, 10 December 1819, in Cappon, p. 529; Jefferson to John Holmes, 22 April 1820, Jefferson to the Marquis de Lafayette, 4 November 1823, in Adrienne Koch and William Peden, eds., *The Life and Selected Writings of Thomas Jefferson* (hereafter cited as "Koch and Peden") (New York: Modern Library, 1944), pp. 698-99, 712.

11. Howe, *American Whigs*, pp. 159-60.

12. Adams to Robert J. Evans, 8 June 1819, in John Adams, *The Works of John Adams* (hereafter cited as "*Works*"), ed. Charles Francis Adams (Boston: Charles C. Little and James Brown, 1851) 10: 379-80; Howe, *American Whigs*, p. 244, cf. p. 245.

13. Howe, *American Whigs*, p. 223.

14. Adams to Louisa Adams, 23 December 1819, in "Letterbook," *Microfilms of the John Adams' Papers* (Boston: Massachusetts Historical Society, 1955), reel 124; Adams to Louisa Adams, 13 January and 23 December 1819, reel 124.

15. Koch and Peden, pp. 257-59.

16. Miller, *Wolf*, pp. 75-77.

17. Jefferson to John Adams, 15 August 1820, Cappon, pp. 567-69.

18. Cf. Henry Steele Commager, *Jefferson, Nationalism, and the Enlightenment* (New York: Braziller, 1986), chap. 4.

19. Jefferson to Charles Bellini, 30 September 1785, Koch and Peden, p. 383; Miller, *Wolf*, p. 99.

20. Jefferson to Adams, 8 April 1816, Cappon, p. 467; cf. Jefferson to Adams, 14 October 1816, p. 490.

21. Miller, *Wolf*, p. 44.

22. Jefferson to Jean Baptiste Say, 1 February 1804, Koch and Peden, p. 575; cf. Fifth Annual Message to Congress, 3 December 1805, Merrill D. Peterson (ed.) *The Portable Jefferson* (New York: Penguin Books, 1977), p. 323.

23. Peterson, *Adams and Jefferson*, p. 9.

24. Caroline Robbins, "The Pursuit of Happiness," in Irving Kristol et al., *America's Continuing Revolution: An Act of Conservation* (Washington, D. C.: American Enterprise Institute for Public Policy Research, 1975), p. 135.

25. Jefferson to Thomas Law, 13 June 1814, Koch and Peden, p. 638; Miller, *Wolf*, p. 94.

26. Jefferson to Abigail Adams, November 1786, Cappon, p. 157.

27. Jefferson to Thomas Law, 13 June 1814, Cappon, pp. 639-40.

28. Jefferson to James Monroe, 20 May 1782, Koch and Peden, p. 364.

29. J. W. Cooke, "Jefferson on Liberty," *Journal of the History of Ideas* 34 (1973): 575.

30. Ibid, p. 575; quoted from Jefferson to Isaac J. Tiffany, 4 April 1819, in Edward Dumbauld, ed., *The Political Writings of Thomas Jefferson: Representative Selections*, American Heritage Series (Indianapolis: Bobbs-Merrill, 1955), p. 55.

31. Jefferson to Thomas Mann Randolph, 30 May 1790, Koch and Peden, p. 496.

32. Lance Banning, *The Jeffersonian Persuasion* (Ithaca, N.Y.: Cornell University Press, 1978), p. 274.

33. Inauguration Address, 4 March 1801, Koch and Peden, p. 322.

34. Miller, *Wolf*, p. 133.

35. Ibid., pp. 15, 37; Phillip Greven, *The Protestant Temperament: Patterns of Childrearing, Religious Experience, and the Self in Early America* (New York: New American Library, 1977), p. 353; "The Autobiography of Thomas Jefferson," 6 January 1821, Koch and Peden, pp. 25-26.

36. "Notes on Virginia," Koch and Peden, p. 272; cf. pp. 252, 255.

37. Cf. Harry V. Jaffa, *Crisis of the House Divided: An Interpretation of the Issues in the Lincoln-Douglas Debates* (Chicago: University of Chicago Press, 1982), pp. 336-37.

38. "Notes on Virginia," Koch and Peden, pp. 256-57.

39. "Autobiography," Koch and Peden, p. 96.

40. Peterson, *Adams and Jefferson*, p. 123.

41. Adams to Jefferson, 15 July 1813, Cappon, p. 358.

42. Cappon, pp. 320-21, 573; "Dissertation on the Canon and Feudal Law" in Adrienne Koch and William Peden, eds., *The Selected Writings of John and John Quincy Adams* (New York: Alfred A. Knopf, 1946), pp. 12-14; Peterson, *Adams and Jefferson*, p. 7.

43. Adams to Jefferson, 14-15 September 1813, Cappon, pp. 375-76.

44. Zoltan Haraszti, *John Adams and the Prophets of Progress* (London: Oxford University Press, 1952), p. 302. Cf. Adams, *Works*, 4: 22.

45. Adams, *Works*, 4: 199; Gilbert Chinard, *Honest John Adams* (Boston: Little, Brown, 1933), p. 90.

46. Adams to Mercy Warren, 25 November 1775, Adams, *Works*, 9: 368.

47. John Adams, *The Diary of John Adams* (14 June 1756), in Adams, *Works*, 1: 33; Adams, *Works*, 4: 97; Cappon, p. 296; Adams, *Works*, 4: 199.

48. Adams, *Works*, 4: 96; cf. Haraszti, *Prophets of Progress*, pp. 144, 147.

49. Adams to John Taylor, 15 April 1814, George A. Peek, Jr., ed., *The Political Writings of John Adams*, (New York: Macmillan, 1954), p. 196.

50. "Discourse on Davila," ibid, p. 197.

51. Adams to Jefferson, 2 March 1816, Cappon, p. 465; cf. Adams to Jefferson, 21 December 1819, Cappon, p. 551; Haraszti, *Prophets of Progress*, p. 77.

52. Adams to Jefferson, 12 May 1820, Cappon, p. 563; cf. Haraszti, *Prophets of Progress*, pp. 66, 106.

53. Haraszti, *Prophets of Progress*, p. 66.

54. Adams, *Works*, 10: 141; cf. p. 147.

55. Adams to Jefferson, 25 December 1813, Cappon, p. 412.

56. Haraszti, *Prophets of Progress*, pp. 71-72.

57. Linda K. Kerber, *Federalists in Dissent: Imagery and Ideology in Jeffersonian America* (Ithaca, N.Y.: Cornell University Press, 1970).

58. Adams to Jefferson, 29 June 1778, Cappon, p. 10; and Adams to Jefferson, 25 June 1813, Cappon, p. 334.

59. L. H. Butterfield, *The Book of Abigail and John: Selected Letters of the Adams Family, 1762-1784* (Cambridge: Harvard University Press, 1975), p. 120.

60. Koch and Peden, *Writings of John and John Quincy Adams*, John Quincy Adams to John Adams, 29 October 1816, pp. 289-91; 3 January 1817, pp. 291-92; *The Diary of John Quincy Adams* (3 March 1820), ed. Allen Nevins (New York: Frederick Ungar, 1969), pp. 230-32.

61. Adams to John Taylor, Peek, *Political Writings*, p. 207; Miller, *Wolf*, p. 258.

62. Adams to Jefferson, 22 January 1825, Cappon, p. 607; cf. Adams to Jefferson, 15 September 1813, Cappon, p. 376.

63. By very different routes some of my colleagues have reached a similar conclusion. Whether we find radical, apolitical individualism to proceed ultimately from Jefferson, as Robert Bellah seems to hold (which would also be my view), from the protestant conscience, as Michael Walzer claims, or more immediately, as Robert Calvert holds, from the Progressive era, I sense an agreement that such a view is incapable of supporting either a democratic citizenship or a coherent political life.

3

CITIZENSHIP, DIVERSITY, AND THE SEARCH FOR THE COMMON GOOD

ROBERT N. BELLAH

The motto *e pluribus unum* appeared on the Great Seal of the United States adopted by Congress in 1782 and clearly referred to the formation of one nation out of thirteen states. The Preamble to the Constitution, speaking in the name of the people, gives as its first purpose "to form a more perfect union." Certainly there were many concerned with the protection of the diversity symbolized in the notion of states' rights—they were prominent among the opponents of the new Constitution—but the Constitution itself emphasizes the *unum* more than the *e pluribus*. Perhaps this primary concern with unity was inevitable in the infancy of a still fragile republic that would face threats of dissolution for many decades. Our situation is quite different. The American nation faces many problems, but dissolution into its constituent states is probably not one of them. Under these circumstances anxiety about the protection of diversity is more salient in the minds of many than worries about unity. The commonest contemporary term for diversity is pluralism. Our culture is pluralistic, and that pluralism, we are told, is in need of nurture and encouragement.

In this context the "search for the common good," which is my central concern here, may even sound threatening. I know from previous experience that many will find the very idea of the common good problematic in a pluralist society. They will object that there can be no quest for the common good in a pluralist society because there can be no common good in a pluralist society. The essential critical question is, "Whose common good?" or, more belligerently, "Who are you to talk about the common good?" Won't any notion of the common good be just some particular idea reflecting the interests of some particular group trying to force itself on the rich diversity of American pluralism?

In meeting this objection I must develop what I take to be a defensible idea of pluralism that is compatible with the notion of the search for the common good. In so doing I will attempt to distinguish this defensible idea of pluralism from what I believe are two inadequate versions of it.

In one of its versions pluralism is almost synonymous with individualism. Not only society as a whole but every group and every subgroup is said to be pluralistic, and the logical conclusion of that line of thought is to reduce society to its constituent individuals. After all, are we not, each of us, indelibly different? That is one of the deepest beliefs of our society. It is just this kind of individualistic pluralism that can provide the basis for a radical rejection of the idea of the common good by mounting an attack on the good itself. Thomas Hobbes in *Leviathan* argued that there is no Good in itself but only the goods of individuals. The idea of the Good always involves the idea of a right way of life — a life lived together and enacted in common practices that are good in themselves. Such ideas were seen as oppressive by some early modern social thinkers who preferred to think of individuals pursuing personal advantage, goods, interests. Society, they argued, will be torn apart by sectarian warfare if we try to establish the common good, but if we try more modestly to regulate the pursuit of interest and leave morality to the inner life of individuals, then we can have a peaceful society. John Locke drove the point home toward the end of the seventeenth century, concluding, in his *Letter Concerning Toleration*, that religion was a private matter and of no legitimate concern of public authority.[1] In this tradition the idea of "the common good" is replaced by the idea of "the public interest," which turns out to be not something good in itself but merely the sum of all the private interests.

Now the problem with this individualistic notion of pluralism, what I would call shallow pluralism (for example, the *Wall Street Journal* review of *Habits of the Heart*, which argued that people obey traffic lights, the credit system works, what's the problem? Who needs community?), is that it has never described what we are really like. Indeed it is doubtful if a society based on interest alone could even exist. Stephen Douglas, in his great debate with Abraham Lincoln over whether slavery should be extended to the new states being formed from the territories, took the line of the public interest. If the people want slavery, let them have it — one simply sums individual interests. But Lincoln asked whether the interest was morally defensible or not. If slavery is absolutely wrong, then it is tragic that it is permitted in the Constitution, but it certainly must not be allowed to spread to new states, regardless of what the population in those states might wish.[2] Here we have a strong notion of good opposing a strong notion of interest, and even though the good has not always won in American politics we have never been allowed to forget the necessity to seek it.

The second inadequate notion of pluralism is what I would call communalist pluralism. It is less likely than individualist pluralism to criticize the idea of the good or even the common good except at the level of the society as a whole. Each community is seen as having its own idea of its own common good, radically different from the idea of other communities. If individualistic pluralism sees society as a limited contract entered into by individuals to maximize their self-interest, communalist pluralism sees society as resting on uneasy treaty relations between communities so autonomous as virtually to be subnations.

People who think of pluralism in communalist terms have a variety of communities in mind. Often these are racial or ethnic, such as the Black community or the Japanese-American community. Sometimes they are religious, such as the Evangelical community or the Catholic community. The word "community" is used so loosely in America that in recent years it has appeared in such expressions as "the gay community." Even women are sometimes spoken of as a community.

But there is a serious question of what community means in any of these expressions. Often people have in the back of their minds a rather romantic idea of the old ethnic communities in our larger eastern cities, where recent immigrants collected in close proximity to each other and maintained a whole set of institutions, churches, clubs, newspapers, and a wide variety of commercial establishments, often using the native language. Today in cities like Los Angeles we can see Korean or Vietnamese communities that approximate this type.

Yet in America such geographically-bounded communities have usually been transient. Most of the older ethnic groups can no longer be located in specific neighborhoods, or such concentrations are small remnants of what was formerly the dominant pattern. A student of mine studying "the Japanese-American community" in San Francisco discovered that almost no Japanese live in Japantown anymore. With the exception of a couple of retirement homes, most Japanese have moved to middle-class neighborhoods in San Francisco or to the suburbs. What was once Japantown is now the location of the Japanese Cultural Center and a collection of shops, restaurants, and cultural institutions, many of them financed with Japanese rather than Japanese-American money. Even blacks, subjected to a segregation more systematic and stringent than any other group, have moved in large numbers out of the ghettos, which in consequence are the depopulated and impoverished fragments of what they once were.

In *Habits of the Heart* we tried to give the much abused term "community" a concise and coherent meaning. We defined it thus: A community is a group of people who are socially interdependent, who participate together in discussion and decision making, and who share certain practices that both define the community and are nurtured by it. We differentiated what we called communities in the strong sense, as just defined, from what we call life-style enclaves, composed of people who share patterns of dress, consumption, and leisure activities but who are not interdependent, do not make decisions together, and do not share a common history. Many groups that are called communities in America are really closer to life-style enclaves, including some of those I have mentioned above.[3]

But even the strongest communities seldom if ever meet the definition that is implied by the idea of communalist pluralism. For true examples of the latter we would have to go to Northern Ireland or Lebanon. There we do indeed find communities that are subnations, radical in their separateness, and in latent or actual armed conflict with their neighbors. In such situations loyalty to the communal group is absolute. It is only there that a common good exists; there is no sense of a common good in the larger society, or that sense has become so submerged as to be inaccessible. We have had such instances in America, but they are not normal. The most striking example divided us into two nations, one slave holding and one free, and led to the Civil War. But there are a few others: the Mormons in their early history, certain groups of radical survivalists in rural America today, and the American Indians, but the latter is a special case that I will consider later. If groups that meet the full definition of communalist pluralism are rare and transient, then we can see that communalist pluralism is an inadequate expression of the reality of pluralism in America.

Having disposed of the two inadequate notions of pluralism, how can we define a defensible conception? What we need is a notion of plural communities that are not easily decomposed into their constituent individuals but that are far from total in their demands;

that have boundaries but that encourage a good deal of give and take across those boundaries. Such an idea of community is possible because all of us belong to more than one community and there is no community to which we belong exclusively without having some of our roles outside of it. This means that we are constantly shifting between being insiders and outsiders with respect to all the significant communities to which we belong. In principle that allows for openness and flexibility. It may, however, tempt us to think of ourselves as disengaged individuals, only tenuously and voluntarily connected to any community.

It is only in complex societies that the notion of multiple and flexible community membership becomes possible, and it is not until modern times that such an idea becomes fully legitimate. In tribal societies and in premodern complex societies, all-encompassing community membership was the norm. Modern nationalism emerged at a unique moment in the history of communal identities. It served to break the hold of the traditional particularistic communities of kinship, region, and religion, but it substituted an identity that could be as absolute in its demands as any traditional one. While nationalism remains a powerful force everywhere in the world, including in our own country, its excesses have brought it into disrepute and subjected it to searching criticism. We can differentiate between patriotism, which is love of country, and nationalism, which is idolatrous worship of country. We can be patriotic while asserting many loyalties that transcend the nation, such as to religion, science, and art, and that involve us in quite concrete communities that are international in scope. Yet disillusionment with nationalism may serve only to disaggregate people into private and transient loyalties.

In short the third conception of pluralism for which I am arguing is difficult to maintain and involves balancing between the conflicting pull toward radical individualism on the one hand and absolutist communalism on the other. Perhaps some historical examples might be helpful in clarifying the issues.

We might begin with a look at how the founders of our country saw the problem of unity and diversity. We have already seen that *e pluribus unum* meant in the first instance the creation of one nation out of thirteen colonies, each of which had its own particular history for a hundred or a hundred and fifty years before independence and had learned to work together only in the crisis of independence itself. There were differences in their economies, the degree to which they depended on agriculture, slave agriculture, commerce, fishing, and shipping. Some New England colonies had Congregational establishments, some southern colonies had Anglican establishments, and the middle colonies had no religious establishments at all. But among the various forms of diversity that had to be reconciled, the one that we would think of first, cultural diversity arising from a multiethnic, multiracial population, was not prominent in the thinking of the founding generation. For one thing there was not much ethnic diversity among the white population, although there were Dutch in New York and Germans in Pennsylvania. Nor, by contrast with European societies, was colonial America a class-divided society. Assimilating relatively small numbers of northwest Europeans in an overwhelmingly Anglo-Saxon white population of the "middling rank" was not viewed as a major problem.

On the other hand racial diversity was seen more as a threat to unity than a creative challenge to it. Although there were a few voices raised in favor of the emancipation of the slaves already in the late eighteenth century, there was little reflection on the inclusion of blacks in a genuinely multiracial society. Southerners, like Jefferson, who opposed slavery in principle but could not see how the issue was to be resolved practically, thought ultimately the resolution would come only through radical separation, either a return of blacks to Africa or the establishment of separate political entities here. In the North segregation was considered the only acceptable solution. A similar solution was assumed in relation to Indians, whose status as separate nations was accepted in principle. However, these nations were constantly required to move westward as their more immediately accessible lands were desired by white settlers. In the 1830s America was so little a multiracial society in the sense of unity in diversity that Alexis de Tocqueville, in the longest and gloomiest chapter in *Democracy in America*, predicted a war of racial extermination between the three races as the only solution to the racial problem in America. We may be glad that Tocqueville, who was right in so many of his predictions, was wrong in that one.[4]

It is commonly assumed that the inability to accept racial and cultural diversity and to develop a positive sense of pluralism derived from communal absolutism. For example, it was the arrogant assumption of the superiority of Anglo-Saxon race and culture that made white Americans unwilling to include others in a genuinely multiracial, multicultural society. I would suggest that radical individualism was just as inhospitable to the acceptance of genuine difference. Let me give an example.

Jefferson's views on slavery and blacks are too complex and too controversial to be dealt with briefly,[5] but his views on American Indians are simpler. Jefferson had great respect for the Indian peoples. Some of his addresses to Indian leaders are quite moving. As president he did what he could to ensure that Indians were treated with justice and their claims legally recognized. But two paragraphs of his Second Inaugural Address are most revealing:

> The aboriginal inhabitants of these countries I have regarded with the commiseration their history inspires. Endowed with the faculties and rights of men, breathing an ardent love of liberty and independence, and occupying a country which left them no desire but to be undisturbed, the stream of overflowing population from other regions directed itself on these shores; without power to divert, or habits to contend against, they have been overwhelmed by the current, or driven before it; now reduced within limits too narrow for the hunter's state,[6] humanity enjoins us to teach them agriculture and the domestic arts; to encourage them to that industry which alone can enable them to maintain their place in existence, and to prepare them in time for that state of society, which to bodily comforts adds the improvement of the mind and morals. We have therefore liberally furnished them with the implements of husbandry and household use; we have placed among them instructors in the arts of first necessity; and they are covered with the aegis of the law against aggressors from among ourselves.[7]

We may be already uneasy at Jefferson's confidence in the rightness of attempting to turn Indians into yeoman farmers of the sort he thought were the backbone of the American republic. But the next paragraph is alarming indeed:

> But the endeavors to enlighten them on the fate which awaits their present course of life, to induce them to exercise their reason, follow its dictates, and change their pursuits with the change of circumstances, have powerful obstacles to encounter; they are combated by the habits of their bodies, prejudice of their minds, ignorance, pride, and the influence of interested and crafty individuals among them, who feel themselves something in the present order of things, and fear to become nothing in any other. These persons inculcate a sanctimonious reverence for the customs of their ancestors; that whatsoever they did, must be done through all time; that reason is a false guide,

and to advance under its counsel, in their physical, moral, or political condition, is perilous innovation; that their duty is to remain as their Creator made them, ignorance being safety, and knowledge full of danger; in short, my friends, among them is seen the action and counteraction of good sense and bigotry; they, too, have their anti-philosophers, who find an interest in keeping things in their present state, who dread reformation, and exert all their faculties to maintain the ascendancy of habit over the duty of improving our reason, and obeying its mandates.[8]

In this paragraph Jefferson reveals a complete antipathy to traditional Indian culture, whose communal conception of landholding consistently opposed the notion of dividing tribal land into individual family farms and succeeding in the world on the basis of individual enterprise. But Jefferson's antipathy is not based on any alleged superiority of Anglo-Saxon race or traditional culture. Rather it is based on the rejection by the Indians of the ideas of reason and progress as Jefferson understood them.

Interestingly enough this passage had a double meaning. There is no reason to believe that Jefferson did not mean what he said to apply to the Indians. But its more salient and only thinly disguised intent was to attack the New England Federalists and particularly the New England clergy whom he saw as standing behind them. Jefferson had rejoiced at the near destruction of the Episcopal church in Virginia following disestablishment there and looked forward to a similar result once the last remnants of establishment (not outlawed at the state level by the first amendment) were eliminated in Massachusetts and Connecticut. So it was the New England clergy who were the crafty medicine men, holding their people in the thrall of ignorance, bigotry, and ancestral custom and opposing innovation, reason, and progress.[9]

It may come as a shock to learn that Jefferson's views on religious freedom involved no love of religious diversity. Jefferson was an early example of what could be called a religious individualist—he said, for example, "I am a sect myself"—and he believed his views were based on reason and free inquiry. Rejecting what he called the "demoralizing dogmas of Calvin," he advocated Unitarianism in theology, which he hoped would soon replace all other religious beliefs. "I rejoice," he wrote in 1822, "that in this blessed country of free inquiry and belief, which has surrendered its creed and conscience to neither kings nor priests, the genuine doctrine of one only God is re-

neither kings nor priests, the genuine doctrine of one only God is reviving, and I trust that there is not a *young man* now living in the United States who will not die an Unitarian." His hostility was particularly directed toward Presbyterians (among whom he included New England Congregationalists), of whom he writes,

> Their ambition and tyranny would tolerate no rival if they had power. Systematical in grasping at an ascendancy over all other sects, they aim, like the Jesuits, at engrossing the education of the country, are hostile to every institution which they do not direct, and jealous at seeing others begin to attend at all to that object. The diffusion of instruction, to which there is now so growing an attention, will be the remote remedy to this fever of fanaticism; while the more proximate one will be the progress of Unitarianism. That this will, ere long, be the religion of the majority from north to south, I have no doubt.[10]

Denouncing the fanaticism of his opponents, he nonetheless looked forward to that "ascendancy" of his own views "over all other sects" which he accused them of desiring. Jefferson would be quick to point out the difference. The Calvinists and Jesuits are characterized by priestcraft, creeds, and confessions of faith, whereas his Unitarianism keeps "within the pale of common sense" of the enlightened individual.[11] Yet it is just the community-forming capacity of religion, its rootedness in traditional practices and its nurturance by trained specialists, that Jefferson would undermine, whether among his fellow citizens or among the Indian tribes.[12]

Jefferson's individualism was tempered by a residual Christianity—he did believe in the moral teachings of Jesus and in the Golden Rule—and by his republicanism, his belief that citizens must act together for the common good. But his complex intelligence also embraced a strong dose of individualistic liberalism, as in his views on religion, that would grow progressively stronger in succeeding generations. It is interesting to observe Jeffersonian themes in the great apostle of American individualism, Ralph Waldo Emerson.

Emerson's religious individualism was so radical that he found even Unitarianism too confining and celebrated the essentially solitary spiritual quest of every individual. Like Jefferson he strongly contrasted tradition and innovation. Indeed he saw American culture as divided by a schism between "the party of the Past and the party of the Future," or, as he sometimes called them, the parties of

knowing which side Emerson was on. He tells us to "desert the tradition" because "The perpetual admonition of nature to us, is, 'The world is new, untried. Do not believe the past. I give you the universe a virgin to-day.' "[13] Perhaps nothing in all American literature has had a greater influence on our culture than Emerson's single essay "Self-Reliance," which spells out the individualistic creed and advises us to stand loose to involvement in any community. As the relentless credo of individualism grew ever stronger in America from the late nineteenth century on, it is easy to see how the idea of the common good became harder and harder to understand. Only the summing of individual goods was intelligible, and by the middle of the twentieth century that gave rise to the public opinion poll, itself a misnomer, for it merely sums private opinions and substitutes for, rather than encourages, the development of a genuine public opinion.

Fortunately individualism never dominated the entire field. Not only did the older churches have a stronger doctrine of our social nature than Jefferson or Emerson would have agreed with, but just as Emerson was beginning to write, millions of Catholic immigrants arrived, bringing with them a clearer understanding of social solidarity and the common good than that of even the most Calvinist of Protestants. Yet among the most significant voices raised in this discussion toward the end of the nineteenth century and the beginning of the twentieth was that of the philosopher Josiah Royce, who developed the most articulate philosophy of community that we have yet seen in America.

Although Royce does not mention Emerson in this connection, it is possible that he was influenced by Emerson's terminology when he spoke of communities of memory and of hope. But Royce does not speak of a schism between the two parties; rather he sees memory and hope as belonging together in any healthy conception of community. He begins one of his major books, *The Philosophy of Loyalty*, by commenting on just such attitudes toward the past as Emerson's. "One of the most familiar traits of our time is the tendency to revise tradition, to reconsider the foundations of old beliefs, and sometimes mercilessly to destroy what once seemed indispensable."[14] Royce accepts the inevitability of criticism yet seeks to discover

the true meaning that was latent in the old traditions. Those traditions were often better in spirit than the fathers knew. . . . Revision does not mean mere destruction. We can often say to tradition: That which thou sowest is not quickened except it die. . . . Let us bury the natural body of tradition. What we want is its glorified body and its immortal soul.[15]

What Royce advocates is the life of a community rooted in memory, reverent yet critical of the past, and expectant of the future, cherishing not a blind hope but a hope nurtured by reflection and interpretation. What he fears is what he calls "the individualism of the detached individual, the individualism of the man who belongs to no community which he loves and to which he can devote himself with all his heart, and his soul, and his mind, and his strength." That sort of individualism has "never saved men and never can save men. For mere detachment, mere self-will, can never save men. What saves us on any level of human life is union." Yet Royce is averse to communal absolutism. A tendency to make absolute any community, for example the national community, he equates with the individualism of the detached individual. For a community that does not see itself as part of other communities behaves like a detached individual. Ultimately for Royce all communities come together in what he calls "the great community" or "the beloved community," which is the human race, seen in a religious perspective. It is interesting in this connection to see Royce speaking out in 1905 in his essay "Race Questions and Prejudices," opposing the "scientific" racism so prominent in his day and defending the dignity of Asians and blacks. He concludes the essay by writing, "For my part, then, I am a member of the human race, and this is a race which is, as a whole, considerably lower than the angels, so that the whole of it very badly needs race-elevation. In this need of my race I personally and very deeply share. And it is in this spirit only that I am able to approach our problem."[16]

Just as Royce saw vigorous and effective individuals strengthening communities, so he saw strong and effective communities strengthening larger societies. He lamented the decline of local loyalties in America and offered the notion of "provincialism," not in a pejorative but in a positive sense, as an antidote. He thought a vigorous provincialism would strengthen national life, not weaken it, for he believed that genuine communities, oriented toward past and future, living out of memory and hope, are communities of interpreters capable of communicating with other such communities in search of the common good.[17]

It has been difficult to maintain continuity with ideas such as those of Royce in the twentieth century. John Dewey already in the

those of Royce in the twentieth century. John Dewey already in the 1920s lamented the decline of a genuine public which he understood in terms not far from Royce as a community capable of discourse about the common good.[18] Instead we have seen the rise of what Alasdair MacIntyre calls "bureaucratic individualism."[19] This is an individualism less heroic than Emerson's, resigned to the pursuit of private good within the large, bureaucratic structures that generally dominate our society. Bureaucratic individualism produces a public discourse dominated by experts and technocrats arguing about who has more effective means to increase economic productivity and national power. These means need no end to justify them; it is assumed that they will increase the sum of individual benefits. Yet our best minds have frequently pointed out the poverty of an understanding of public life as the quest for private benefits modulated by bureaucratic management. Walter Lippmann, writing in 1955, spoke of "the hollow shell of freedom." He said that "the citadel is vacant because the public philosophy is gone, and all that the defenders of freedom have to defend in common is a public neutrality and a public agnosticism."

In 1962 John Courtney Murray offered a stunning judgment:[20]

And if this country is to be overthrown from within or from without, I would suggest that it will not be overthrown by Communism. It will be overthrown because it will have made an impossible experiment. It will have undertaken to establish a technological order of most marvelous intricacy, which will have been constructed and will operate without relations to true political ends: and this technological order will hang, as it were, suspended over a moral confusion; and this moral confusion will itself be suspended over a spiritual vacuum. This would be the real danger resulting from a type of fallacious, fictitious fragile unity that could be created among us.[21]

Certainly American society in the twenty-five years since Murray wrote those words has shown many symptoms of moral confusion and spiritual vacuum. In the late sixties and early seventies our society was torn apart by controversy over our involvement in a war whose means seemed far more terrible than any attainable end could justify. Then we underwent the unprecedented experience of events leading up to the resignation of a president, who otherwise would have been impeached, and the sordid tale of the unscrupulous manipulation of power that was revealed at that time. By the

institutions was at an all-time low. And only ten years later we went through a similar experience. Under an administration that came into office asserting that the period of national doubt was over, we witnessed a new wave of doubt whose implications we cannot yet fathom. In the fall of 1984, President Reagan, on the floor of the New York Stock Exchange, declared that "this is the age of the individual, this is the age of the entrepreneur." It was part of the ethos of that administration to legitimate a spirit of private acquisition such as we had not seen in many decades, and when the harvest came in it was evident in the daily newspaper headlines. It would seem that Ivan Boesky was only the first of many members of our highest financial circles who put private greed above fiduciary responsibility. Nor was the age of the individual and the entrepreneur confined to the stock exchange. Apparently there were those in the White House who would have run our government in that fashion. President Reagan's admiration for Oliver North suggested that North's failings and those of his confederates were not merely private weaknesses of their own.

But while that administration encouraged the spirit of what Royce called "the individualism of the detached individual" to a unique degree, it simultaneously saw fit to encourage the revival of communal absolutism on the part of the Christian right. And so we saw on the public stage proposals for a "Christian America" with an agenda not open to public discussion but pursued with triumphalist self-righteousness. Headlines of the day suggested that even the heartland of religious communal absolutism is not immune to the entrepreneurial power plays that led to disgrace in Wall Street and the White House. Yet what we did not see, between rampant individualism on the one hand and communal absolutism on the other, is anything that Lippmann or Murray would have recognized as a public philosophy concerned with the common good.

It was in hope of reviving a discussion concerning a public philosophy, of reinvigorating traditions that can still speak to us, and of encouraging the communities of memory and hope that are still to be found among us that my four coauthors and I published *Habits of the Heart*. Many of our academic colleagues have assured us that our effort was vain. The forum is empty and the voices are stilled they tell us. Or they worry that our sympathy for communities of memory, such as the family and the church, will only encourage regressive patriarchalism and fundamentalist bigotry. They did not see that our attitude toward tradition was that of Royce: not unthinking acceptance, but active and critical reappropriation. And perhaps they did not appreciate our position because they too are devoted to the individualism of the detached individual. What could be more detached than the assertion of the critical intellectual that there is no hope for America?

Yet in spite of much criticism and many doubts we have been heartened by the wide variety of groups actively involved in American life who have found our work helpful. These include civic groups, charitable groups, labor and business groups, but above all religious groups, and from an extraordinarily wide spectrum: American Indians, Buddhists, Jews, Catholics, mainline Protestants, and Evangelicals. This is not surprising, for among the communities of memory and hope in America religious groups take a prominent place. Nor do most of them, including most Evangelicals, see themselves as communal absolutists. Rather, they would be prepared to accept Reinhold Niebuhr's conception of the role of religious groups in American life. Niebuhr spoke of a "religious solution of the problem of religious diversity":

> This solution makes religious and cultural diversity possible within the presuppositions of a free society, without destroying the religious depth of culture. The solution requires a very high form of religious commitment. It demands that each religion, or each version of a single faith, seek to proclaim its highest insights while yet preserving an humble and contrite recognition of the fact that all actual expressions of religious faith are subject to historical contingency and relativity. . . . Religious toleration through religiously inspired humility is always a difficult achievement. It requires that religious convictions be sincerely and devoutly held while yet the sinful and finite corruptions of these convictions be humbly acknowledged; and the actual fruits of other faiths be generously estimated.[22]

In that spirit, each religious community brings the insight of its own tradition to bear on our common problems while remaining open to discussion and persuasion by others who bring different insights. I would like to close with one example to show that this Roycean conception of diversity, what we might call deep pluralism, is not dead: The example of the American Catholic bishops' pastoral letter "Economic Justice for All." The pastoral letter draws on the Bible, the church fathers, and modern Catholic social teaching to address critical issues in our economic life today. The letter does not offer dogmatic solutions to particular problems but calls for further discussion and judicious action with respect to them. But rather than the particular policy recommendations, what I want to discuss here briefly is the fundamental framework of the letter which expresses so eloquently the argument I am trying to make.

The letter asserts firmly that "Human life is life in Community." It roots this teaching in the most central tenets of Christian faith, in Jesus's commandments to love God with all one's heart and one's neighbor as oneself. Indeed it finds community central to the trinitarian conception of God as the very focus of Christian belief. And it draws from this fundamental belief an inescapable norm for social life: "Human dignity, realized in community with others and with the whole of God's creation, is the norm against which every social institution must be measured." From the norm flows the obligation to perform personal acts of charity by individuals, families, and the church itself. But the norm is not exhausted by personal acts of charity. The bishops argue for the importance of citizenship as an essential expression of the norm:

> The virtues of citizenship are an expression of Christian love more crucial in today's interdependent world than ever before. These virtues grow out of a lively sense of one's dependence on the commonweal and obligations to it. This civic commitment must also guide the economic institutions of society. In the absence of vital sense of citizenship among the businesses, corporations, labor unions, and other groups that shape economic life, society as a whole is endangered. Solidarity is another name for this social friendship and civic commitment that make human moral and economic life possible.[23]

I am not a Roman Catholic but an active member of another communion, yet I and others like me have been involved with the letter both in the hearings that led up to it and in discussions that have followed. In this letter we have an example of a community of memory and hope, drawing on its own deepest resources but opening up a discussion in fellowship with other citizens about the common good. If this discussion, and others like it, can broaden and eventuate in lively debates that will affect policy decisions, then there is still hope for us as citizens of America and of the larger world. The letter and the process it has stimulated are exemplary in showing us how we can draw on our diversity to nourish the virtues of citizenship in pursuit of the common good.

NOTES

1. Locke believed he had "proved that the care of souls does not belong to the magistrate. . . . The care, therefore, of every man's soul belongs unto himself, and is to be left unto himself." *Treatise of Civil Government and a Letter Concerning Toleration* (New York: Appleton-Century-Crofts, 1937), pp. 186–87.

2. The Lincoln-Douglas debates can be found in Abraham Lincoln, *Speeches and Writings, 1832–1858*, ed. Don E. Fehrenbacher (New York: Library of America, 1989).

3. Robert N. Bellah et al., *Habits of the Heart: Individualism and Commitment in American Life* (Berkeley and Los Angeles: University of California Press, 1985), pp. 333–35.

4. Alexis de Tocqueville, *Democracy in America*, trans. George Lawrence, ed. J. P. Mayer (Garden City, N.Y.: Doubleday, 1969), 1: pt. 2, chap. 10.

5. See David Greenstone's extensive discussion of this issue on pp. 20–32.

6. Jefferson accepts the myth of the Indians as hunters without realizing that most of those in the eastern states were primarily agriculturalists.

7. Thomas Jefferson, *Writings*, ed. Merrill D. Peterson (New York: Library of America, 1984), p. 520.

8. Ibid., pp. 520–21.

9. See Henry Adams, *History of the United States of America During the Administration of Thomas Jefferson, 1801–1809*, ed. Earl N. Harbert (New York: Library of America, 1986), pp. 606–7.

10. Fortunately Jefferson did not live to see his beloved University of Virginia headed by a theologically conservative Presbyterian minister.

11. Jefferson, *Writings*, pp. 1459, 1464.

12. Jefferson's legacy is to be seen in the wholesale rejection by frontier Christianity in the nineteenth century of the ideal of an educated clergy and in the reliance of evangelicalism on what Richard Hofstadter called the "religion of the heart." See his *Anti-Intellectualism in American Life* (New York: Alfred A. Knopf, 1963), pt. 2.

13. Ralph Waldo Emerson, *Essays and Lectures*, ed. Joel Porte (New York: Library of America, 1983), pp. 100–101.

14. Josiah Royce, *The Philosophy of Loyalty* (New York: Macmillan Co., 1918), p. 3.

15. Ibid., pp. 11–12.

16. *The Basic Writings of Josiah Royce*, ed. John J. McDermott (Chicago: University of Chicago Press, 1969), 2:1154, 1110.

17. Royce, *Philosophy of Loyalty*, pp. 245–48. See also "Provincialism," in *Basic Writings of Josiah Royce*, 2:1067–88, and Josiah Royce, *The Problem of Christianity* (Chicago: University of Chicago Press, 1968).

18. See John Dewey, *The Public and Its Problems* (Chicago: Henry Holt, 1927), chap. 4.

19. See Alasdair MacIntyre, *After Virtue* (Notre Dame, Ind.: University of Notre Dame Press, 1981), p. 33.

20. Walter Lippmann, *The Public Philosophy* (New York: Mentor Books, 1955), p. 88.

21. John Courtney Murray, "Return to Tribalism," *Catholic Mind* 60 (January 1962): 5-12, as cited in Richard John Neuhaus, *The Naked Public Square* (Grand Rapids, Mich.: Eerdmans, 1984), p. 85.

22. Reinhold Niebuhr, *The Children of Light and the Children of Darkness* (New York: Scribner's, 1944), pp. 134-35, 137-38.

23. U. S. Catholic Bishops' Pastoral Letter, *Economic Justice for All: Catholic Social Teaching and the U. S. Economy* (13 November 1986), paragraphs 25, 63, 64, and 66, *Origins* 16 (27 November 1986): 415, 419.

4

"IN COMMON TOGETHER": UNITY, DIVERSITY, AND CIVIC VIRTUE

JEAN BETHKE ELSHTAIN

I

The question of the one and the many, of unity and diversity, has been posed since the beginning of political thought in the West. The American Founders were well aware of the vexations attendant upon the creation of a new political body. They worked with, and against, a stock of metaphors that had previously served as the symbolic vehicles of political incorporation. As men of the Enlightenment, they rejected the images of the body politic that had dominated medieval and early modern political thinking. For a Jefferson or a Madison such tropes as "the King's two bodies" or John of Salisbury's twelfth-century rendering, in his *Policraticus*, of a body politic with the Prince as the head and animating force of other members were too literalist, too strongly corporatist, and too specifically Christian to serve the *novus ordo saeculorum*. But they were nonetheless haunted by Hebrew and Christian metaphors of a covenanted polity: The body is one but has many members. There is, there can be, unity with diversity.

Indeed, one could even go so far as to insist that it is incorporation, enfolding, within a single body that makes meaningful diversity possible. Our differences must be recognized if they are to exist substantively at all. We cannot be "different" all by ourselves. A political body that simultaneously brings persons together, creating a "we," but enables these same persons to separate themselves and to recognize one another in and through their differences as well as in

My thanks to Robert Calvert for his meticulous editing and perceptive criticisms as this essay was in progress.

what they share in common—that was the great challenge. If debates in recent years between the individualist and communitarian positions, as these have been tagged, are any indication, the problems generated by the need for unity that goes beyond mere "law and order," as well as the quest for diversity that goes beyond mere "tolerance," have become ever more acute. There is, then, an unresolved tension embedded in our history and our primary documents between individual rights and immunities and the vision of "we the people."

This ambiguity is inherent in American political culture and has persisted since the founding. It is an ambiguity encoded in the Constitution and the Bill of Rights, in a simultaneous commitment to a "we" and to a protection of the "one," and it is at one and the same time a source of strength and a cause for concern. Current individualist and communitarian debates are *not*, therefore, engagements between traditionalists and antitraditionalists, or between liberals and restorationists. Rather, the intensity of, and interest in, this discussion is best understood as a contestation over the appropriation of tradition itself.[1] The Founders were Enlightenment figures who rejected traditions embodied in monarchical absolutism, but they also thought in some very traditional ways: Natural law and natural right were not their invention. Preoccupied from time to time with classical republican precedents, the Federalists and Anti-Federalists struggled with a general fund of ideas, a repertoire of stock concerns and understandings much as contemporary interlocutors do.

Modern American political culture is neither an à la carte menu nor a fixed dinner. No one among us could participate in all the possibilities contemporary culture spreads before each human subject. Neither is it really workable to be so totally immersed in one fixed mode that no alternative to this conception, this belief, this way of doing things ever presents itself. Total rejection of the entire cultural menu is no genuine alternative either, as defenders of liberal individualism and their critics make clear. Traditions exist; they are never created *de novo*. To "think" a tradition is to bring matters to the surface, to engage in debate with interlocutors long dead or protagonists who never lived save on the page and, through that engagement, to elaborate alternative conceptions through which to apprehend one's political culture and the way that culture represents itself or is represented. The meaning and rationale of the most basic things about us—we the people—as well as each one of us taken singly is at stake.

Thus Robert Bellah in Chapter 3 argues for a vision of community that opposes both radical individualism, on the one hand, and a flattened-out, homogeneous union that obliterates differences, on the other. Michael Walzer reminds us that much of the strength of our tradition is its protesting, separating, even privatizing tendencies, with the Bill of Rights the touchstone of this robust individuating dynamic. We look to a second prong, our "federal" or constitutional tradition, to revitalize associative life, a process open to many abuses and pitfalls. Specifically, according to Walzer, despite "its anticipation of collective action, the Constitution has turned out to favor something else, nicely summed up in the twentieth-century maxim about 'doing your own thing.' "[2] In this essay I begin by building on Bellah's and Walzer's insights but from a somewhat different angle of vision. I go on to offer reflections on an epoch in our history unpacked in Robert Calvert's essay, namely the Progressive Era, which was the point at which a rather loose, federated union moved in the direction of building and justifying the need for a powerful, centralized, bureaucratic order. That, in turn, helps to set the stage for my turn to two evolving traditions — Catholic social thought and the democratic theorizing of civil society emerging from Central Eastern Europe — as sources of insight and strength for American political thinkers who, with me, have grown weary of the stark alternatives, individualism versus collectivism, or choice versus constraint, alternatives all too often presented to us when the philosophic debate over tradition takes actual shape in our political rhetoric and public policy alternatives.

II

A preliminary discussion is needed to frame the horizon for my considerations of the way that the quest for national unity under the auspices of the state has, over time, exercised a corrosive effect on America's regional and localist images of community and, as well, on a once deeply and widely shared, religiously grounded concept of the human person, the "exalted individual," in the words of political theorist Glenn Tinder. Tinder has argued that the idea of an individual whose ontological dignity is such that he or she deserves "attention" and is not to be "grossly violated" is fundamental to the Christian standpoint that is constitutive of our political institutions and culture at its best. Were the horizons of our political life to cease being framed through an insistence that the destiny of each individual matters, that life would become what it now is only in part, "an affair of expediency and self-interest."[3]

This possibility, in turn, invites a focus on *civil society*, by which I mean "the many forms of community and association that are not political in form: families, neighborhoods, voluntary associations of innumerable kinds, labor unions, small business, giant corporations, and religious communities."[4] Some may cavil at the notion that such associations are not "political," but theorists of civil society would insist, in response, that this network and the many ways we are nested within it, lie outside the formal structure of state power. Walzer claims that the Bill of Rights aimed specifically to promote and to protect such associative group rights, not merely or solely individual immunities or entitlements. There is no sharp dichotomy between state and society in this understanding; rather a complex dialectic pertains, or ideally ought to pertain, between the two. State and society are intimately intertwined, at least this is the assumption that guides the most thoughtful constructions of that relationship.

The statist, however, is one who wants us to thin out these ties of civil society and the plural loyalties and diverse imperatives they give rise to and sustain. His citizen is represented as unhesitatingly loyal to the state and prepared to give primacy to it and its purposes in any and all situations. For the statist identifies us primarily as civic creatures available for mobilization by a powerful, centralized mechanism rather than as family men and women, neighbors, members of the Elks Club or a feminist health cooperative, activists trying to save the African elephant from extinction, participants in a reading group, Baptists, and so on. Indeed, statist politicians and philosophies often design programs and policies aimed at destroying alternative loyalties and the containers for identity they provide.

Civil society is a realm that is neither individual in a narrowly relentless individualist sense nor communitarian in a strong collectivist sense. It is that world evoked by the Anti-Federalists in debates over ratification of the United States Constitution. From time to time, Anti-Federalists no doubt pushed an idealized image of a self-contained and self-reliant republic which shunned imperial power and worked, instead, to create a polity modeled on classic principles of civic virtue and a common good. Writes a historian of this argument:

Anti-federalists saw mild, grass-roots, small-scale governments in sharp contrast to the splendid edifice and overweening ambition implicit in the new Constitution — and, indeed, heralded by Publius and its other proponents. The first left citizens free to live their own lives and to cultivate the virtue (private and public) vital to republicanism, while the second soon entailed taxes and drafts and offices and wars damaging to human dignity and thus fatal to self-government.[5]

Despite the often roseate hue with which the Anti-Federalists surrounded their arguments, they were on to something, as we like to say. They hoped to avoid, even to break, a cycle later elaborated by Alexis de Tocqueville in which highly self-interested and motivated individualists disarticulated from the saving constraints and nurture of overlapping associations of social life require more and more checks, balances, and controls "from above" in order that the disintegrative effects of untrammeled individualism be at least somewhat muted in practice.

To this end, the peripheries must remain vital; political spaces other than or beneath (it is almost impossible not to employ spatial metaphors as a kind of lexicon of power-talk) those of the state need to be cherished, nourished, kept vibrant. They had in mind local councils and committees, and they had in mind to avoid concentrations of power at the core or "on the top." Too much centralized power was as bad as no power at all. Only small-scale *civitates* would enable individuals, as citizens, to cultivate authentic civic virtue. For such virtue turns on meaningful participation in a powerful ideal of community. Too much power exercised at a level beyond that which permits, indeed demands, active citizen participation is destructive of civic dignity and, finally, fatal to any authentic understanding of democratic self-government. Anti-Federalist fears of centralized and overnationalized power presaged Tocqueville's later worry that imperial greatness bought through force of arms is "pleasing to the imagination of a democratic people" because it sends out lightning bolts of "vivid and sudden luster, obtained without toil, by nothing but the risk of life."[6]

Tocqueville had another worry, one much debated by political and social theorists: Even as the reality of American democracy freed individuals from the constraints of older, undemocratic structures and obligations, individualism and privatization were also unleashed. Tocqueville's fear was not that this invites anarchy; rather, he believed that the individualism of an acquisitive commercial republic, especially one bent on a course of empire, will engender new forms of social and political domination. All social webs that once held persons intact having disintegrated, the individual finds himself or herself isolated and impotent, exposed and unprotected. Into this power vacuum moves the organized force of government in the form of a top-heavy, centralized state.

This Tocquevillian anxiety has spurred thinkers in the communitarian tradition, whether indebted to Burkean traditionalism or not, to score American individualism and to see its effects as the bane of our times that a more communal ethic must tame or even supplant. I agree with the general contours of this critique, and my work has been associated with this theoretical and political tendency; however, I have a fear of my own spurred by responses to the Tocquevillian scenario adumbrated above. My worry is that critiques of excessive, atomistic, and acquisitive individualism often do not distinguish carefully enough between the phenomenon grasped in the 1980s slogan "greed is good" and the ennobling strengths of our tradition of individuality, of respect for the human person, taken as a single, unique, irreplaceable self.

III

I ask the reader to return with me for just a moment to the Greeks, to that classical world dominated by the ideal of the city-state, the *polis*. One sees a world in which war is construed as the natural state of mankind and an imperious source of communal loyalty and purpose. The Greek city-state was a community of warriors whose political rights were determined by the fundamental privilege of the soldier to decide his own fate, to choose death nobly. There was a direct line of descent from Homeric warrior assemblies to Athenian naval democracy. Citizenship was restricted to those who bore arms. One reigning definition of justice, repeated by Thrasymachus in his sparring with Socrates in the first book of Plato's *Republic*, was "the interest of the stronger." The Greek citizen army was an expression of the Greek *polis*, its creation one of the chief concerns and consequences of the formation of the city-state. In Sparta, the army organized into mess groups was substituted for the family as the basic element of the state. Another custom of the male group, homosexuality, was developed and institutionalized, most systematically at Thebes in the fourth century, to create a sacred band of fraternal lovers fighting side by side. Such institutions served to ensure that fellowship was deemed a prerequisite of disciplined courage in war, of the willingness to risk death together.

The human body in Greek, then Roman, antiquity was wholly conscripted into society, an insight I owe to the great historian of late antiquity, Peter Brown.[7] His is an important point: The pre-Christianized individual was not free to withhold his or her body from conscription into the extant social order. One could with Socrates endorse withdrawal of the soul from the body, but one could not take oneself out of the group—one could not constitute one's body as a protest against its conscription into the social body in the form of warrior, slave, or householder. The classical view is that the city-state should have complete control of human bodies for the purposes of labor, procreation, and war.

The body, hence the self, existed at the behest of the wider social order. St. Augustine argues that Rome perfected the regime of *cupiditas* run rampant, the triumph of a lust to dominate. The distinctive mark of Roman life as a *civitas terrena*, a city of man, was greed and lust for possession that presumed a right of exploitation. This became a foundation for human relationships, warping and perverting personality, marriage, the family, all things. Augustine writes: "For he who desires the glory of possession would feel that his power were diminished, if he were obliged to share it with any living associate. . . he cherishes his own manhood."[8]

The political importance of Christianity, one marked by an impressive array of analysts, critics, and political theorists including Sheldon Wolin, Michael Walzer, Robert Bellah, Gilbert Meilander, and many others, is that Christians created a new vision of community that sanctioned *each* life as well as *everyday* life, especially the lives of society's victims, and granted each a new-found dignity. The warrioring politics of the ancient world found itself put on trial. Writes Tinder: "No one, then, belongs at the bottom, enslaved, irremediably poor, consigned to silence; this is equality. This points to another standard: that no one should be left outside, an alien and a barbarian."[9]

Christianity introduced a strong principle of universalism into the ancient world even as it proclaimed a vision of the "exalted individual," brought into being by a loving creator, not, therefore, the mere creature of any government, any *polis*, any empire. Although early Christians saw themselves as a very particular community, theirs was a community open in principle to all. Had not St. Paul proclaimed that in Christ there is neither Jew nor Greek, free nor slave, male nor female? As early as Monica's death in 387 (Monica, of course, was St. Augustine's indefatigable mother), Christian universalism had taken strong hold. As Monica approaches her death on foreign soil, far away from her city, Carthage, she renounces a "vain desire" to be buried in that soil next to her husband. She is not frightened at leaving her body so far from her own country, for "nothing is far from God, and I need have no fear that he will not know where to find me. . . ."[10] Augustine himself declares, in *The City of God*, that a person's body "belongs to his very nature," and is no "mere adornment, or external convenience."[11] Thus, human beings were not instruments to be put to a civic purpose over which they had no say; rather, persons *qua* persons "deserve attention." There is a minimum standard of care and concern, for every person "has been immeasurably dignified." To be sure, as Tinder almost wearily suggests, this ideal is often "forgotten and betrayed," but "were it erased from our minds our politics would probably become altogether what it is at present only in part—an affair of expediency and self-interest. . . ."[12]

The heady drama of this moral revolution in the ancient world is a story that has lost none of its excitement or importance. The legitimacy once accorded automatically to the claims of the city-state and the empire upon the human body of each person now had to make its case and could not be assumed unproblematically. The human body could withdraw from the demands placed upon it by society. The sexual-social contract could be broken. Freedom of the will could be brought to bear on the body itself as a tangible locus, a sign of a newfound relation of the self to the social world. An elemental freedom was endorsed. Liberated individuals formed communities to validate their newfound *individualities* and to shore up the transformed, symbolically changed good represented by the new social body: The body is one but has many members.

It is important to be clear about the nature of this freedom. The body was not exempt from a self-imposed discipline. To be a member of the faithful, one embraced this discipline as one's own. The aim was to be "truly alive," to slough off the "deadness" of abuse of the body flowing from an ontology of lust and domination. The human will—and the concept of "will" is unknown before Christianity, most importantly St. Augustine—freely imposed a discipline on itself as a visible sign of freedom: freedom from the abuses of one's own time, freedom for involvement in an alternative construction of self *in* community.[13] For Christian thinkers, as Hannah Arendt observes, "Free Choice of the Will" was a "faculty distinct from desire and reason . . ." and Augustine is "the great and original thinker" who posited two active principles, willing and nilling, as constitutive

of "the faculty of Choice, so decisive for the *liberum arbitrium*. . .
to the choice between *velle* and *nolle*, between willing and nilling."[14]

The Christian life was not primarily a solitary life but a communal one. Nevertheless, the principle introduced by Christians is one
in which persons are irreducibly individuals, but this individuality is
exquisitely social. The person is neither absorbed totally into a communal order, having no identity outside its boundaries, nor is he or
she defined wholly apart from the society of others. The Christian
ideal of community not only departs radically from that of the classical city-state, it also challenges the revivification of this ideal of
fraternal order in the civic republican tradition associated most importantly with Machiavelli and Rousseau. Rousseau scorns any particular interest that might block the general will. He lambastes
Christianity as a notion wholly at odds with that of "republic." For
the polity must be as one; the national will must not be divided; citizens must be prepared to defend civic autonomy through force of
arms; whatever puts the individual at odds with himself is a threat to
"la nation une et indivisible." I call the civic republican ideal one of
"armed civic virtue," for the human virtues are given a strong civic
description and culminate in bearing arms for the republic. Although this ideal has never been embraced in any full-blown form in
the United States, in part because of the brakes to its attainment encoded in the Bill of Rights, enlivened in Tocquevillian associations,
and enshrined in Christian ideals of individuality and sociality, we
have flirted with and even witnessed moments of "armed civic virtue" extolled as an ideal of a community coterminous with a great
nation-state unified and speaking with one voice.

IV

Now join me on the shores of the New Land. The Founders have
done their work. Federalist arguments have won the day though
Anti-Federalist fears simmer just beneath the surface of things. By
the nineteenth century, building on the views of such dissenting Puritans as Roger Williams and Anne Hutchinson, the Christian ideal
of the exalted self takes on a solitary profile in the thoughts and
writings of such important celebrants of individual freedom as Thoreau, Emerson, and others. In contrast to the strong Puritan ideal of
a commonwealth, this refurbished American self stands out more
and more in bold relief against a shadowy and less and less distinctive social background. Philip Abbott has elaborated the peculiarly

American ideal of "perfect freedom," the freedom of a self *apart* from community rather than not-wholly-dominated-and-defined-by an overarching civic body. Americans began to celebrate, indeed to privilege personal experience, whether political, social, or sexual, a celebration that involved a highly evolved, romantic reading of both the Lockean and Christian traditions.[15]

This mirror of freedom is held up beautifully, even chillingly, in an essay by Elizabeth Cady Stanton called "The Solitude of the Self." In common with many American thinkers and activists, Stanton embraced a bewildering smorgasbord of different civic and personal philosophies—liberal, republican, utopian, scientific, and nativist—throughout her long life. As did many Americans of her epoch, she praised the free market yet longed for a community of like-minded souls. She is thus both a representative figure and, as one of the movers and shakers of early feminism and the suffrage movement, an exceptional one. As a representative, even quintessential American thinker of the time, she did not break new intellectual ground, nor did she articulate a coherent system of thought that launched new fields of inquiry or altered the way human beings see their world. (Precious few thinkers do, of course.) She is, however, justifiably regarded as a feminist philosopher whose work embodies an eclectic synthesis and often uncritical embrace of philosophies of individualism and social harmony, laissez-faire, and social cooperation.

But when she got down to brass tacks philosophically, Stanton embraced an ideal of almost perfect freedom, framed from the standpoint of a self she declares sovereign. She locates this ideal, correctly on my view, in "the great doctrine of Christianity," namely, "the right of individual conscience and judgement." You will not find an ideal of the sovereign self in "the Roman idea . . . that the individual was made for the State."[16] As a vision of the self alone, hers is a very selective appropriation of "the great doctrine of Christianity." One could, of course, line her up against other Christian thinkers—particularly those in the social gospel tradition—in order to chasten her robust, romantic embrace of the soul alone. But that is beside the point for my purposes. I call upon Stanton as one of the foremothers of contemporary individualism, particularly in its expressivist variation.

The individual is preeminent, first and foremost, Stanton argues, deploying the Robinson Crusoe metaphor to characterize women on their solitary islands. After the sovereign self comes citizenship, then the generic woman, and last the "incidental relations of life, such as

mother, wife, sister, daughter. . . ."[17] But such incidental social relations are not essentially constitutive of self. The self is prior to social
arrangements. She speaks of the self-sovereignty of women and men
and calls human beings solitary voyagers. We come into the world
alone. We go out alone. We "walk alone." We realize "our awful solitude." Life is a "march" and a "battle," and we are all soldiers of the
self who must fight for our own protection. In "the tragedies and tri-
umphs of human experience, each mortal stands alone." Ideally, she
notes almost offhandedly, this complete individual development is
needed for the "general good." The exalted individual is one who
exults in her own solitude, and Christianity's specifically social and
communal features recede.

Stanton's words conjure up a universe stripped of meaning save
what the individual gives to it and its objects. She aims to disenthrall
the self, to disencumber it in the sure and certain hope that a lofty
and invigorating ideal of freedom will be the end result—and re-
dound to the general good. But this admittedly bracing ideal of the
self is too thin to sustain any notion of a social good, of a civic virtue
we experience "in common together" that we cannot know alone.
Because, in Wolin's words, the political is based on a possibility of
commonality, on "our common capacity to share, to share memories
and a common fate," a recognition of our common being is "the natural foundation of democracy," for "we have an equal claim to participate in the cooperative undertakings on which the common life
depends."[18] Stanton attempts to construct commonality based upon
a vision of isolated, Robinson Crusoe, sovereign selves. Her social
project falters for this reason. She failed to see the irony embedded
in proclamations of a totally individualistic ontology that would, she
optimistically trusted, usher in unproblematically a politics of the
common good, a politics of civic virtue.

V

When America entered the twentieth century, she was a society
driven by dreams and fears of rapid industrialization and commercial expansion, dreams and fears of empire, dreams and fears of perfect freedom, dreams and fears of community. I will pick up the
story of these tangled threads and themes in the World War I era
when the siren allure of an overarching, collective civic purpose took
a statist turn that seemed a cure for what ailed the Republic, at least
on the view of those who lamented our excessive diversity. Stanton's

ideal self, together with throngs of diverse immigrants, invited a centralism response. Nationalizing Progressives, disheartened at the messy sprawl that was American life, appropriately outraged at the excesses of corporate capitalism, and desirous of finding some way to forge a unified national will and civic philosophy, saw the coming of World War I, championed by President Woodrow Wilson, as a way to attain at long last a homogeneous, ordered, and rational society. The central organ of Progressive opinion, the *New Republic*, had inveighed against "unassimilable communities," a fear prompted by the enormous surge in immigration during the waning decades of the nineteenth century and the early decades of the twentieth.

"To be great," wrote John R. Commons, a Progressive labor economist, " nation . . . must be of one mind."[19] Walter Lippmann assaulted the "evils of localism" and fretted that American diversity was too great and had become a block in the way of "order, purpose, discipline."[20] Even before Wilson committed American troops to the European war, Lippmann and other Progressives claimed that war would be good for the state. Writes one critic of Lippmann and Progressives in general: "His conception of both [reform and civic good] presupposed a monolithic, static social structure in which a scientific elite directed a docile, relative homogenous public."[21] A unity engineered from the top *must*, argued the nationalizers, triumph over pluralism, diversity, excessive and necessarily backward localisms.

World War I was to be the great engine of social progress with conscription an "effective homogenizing agent in what many regarded as a dangerously diverse society. Shared military service, one advocate colorfully argued, was the only way to 'yank the hyphen' out of Italian-Americans or Polish-Americans or other such imperfectly assimilated immigrants."[22] President Wilson, who had already proclaimed that any "man who carries a hyphen about him carries a dagger that he is ready to plunge into the vitals of this Republic," and who championed universal service as a way to mold a new nation, now thundered in words of dangerously unifying excess:

There are citizens of the United States, I blush to admit, born under other flags but welcomed under our generous naturalization laws to the full freedom and opportunity of America, who have poured the poison of disloyalty into the very arteries of our national life. . . . Such creatures of passion, disloyalty, and anarchy must be crushed out. . . . The hand of our power should close over them at once.[23]

Armed civic virtue had found a home on the shores of the New Land and this mobilized and manipulated common good proved very common indeed.

A few brave, dissenting voices held out against the tide of xenophobic unity championed by academics and politicians alike. Most important among them was Randolph Bourne, who bitterly attacked his old idol and master, John Dewey, for supporting the war and talking blithely of its "social possibilities." His essay on "The State" retains its force nearly fifty years after he left it incomplete at his untimely death during the flu pandemic in the winter of 1918-1919:

> War—or at least modern war waged by a democratic republic against a powerful enemy—seems to achieve for a nation almost all that the most inflamed political idealist could desire. Citizens are no longer indifferent to their Government, but each cell of the body politic is brimming with life and activity. . . . In a nation at war, every citizen identifies himself with the whole, and feels immensely strengthened in that identification.[24]

Bourne championed the "trans-national" state. He yearned for a civic unity, a politics of commonalties, that cherished and celebrated the bracing tonic that perspicuous contrasts offer to the forging of individualities and communities. He called for an experimental ideal where each of us is free to explore in a world of others; where we can act in common together and act singly. Such an ideal is necessarily hostile to any overly robust proclamation of civic virtue that demands a single, overarching collective unity to attain or to sustain its purposes.

VI

If one cherishes and champions individuality—the exalted individual—and community, diversity and unity, what resources are available in our contemporary civic repertoire that push in this complex direction? We—we late-modern or postmodern citizens of the United States—are no longer naive. We have witnessed and are witnessing the corrosive effects of acquisitive individualism as well as those of the hypernationalistic, collective fevers which have occasionally run rampant in our history. With Bourne's saving and healing irony ready to hand, I will conclude this essay with intimations of a chastened version of civic virtue, one that embraces civility as a feature of that virtue yet also endorses, quite heartily, a fractious, even rumbustious politics.

I will draw from two perhaps unlikely sources—Catholic social thought and the theorizing of civil society that has emerged in a rapidly and hearteningly transforming Central Eastern Europe. This move seems to me politically and discursively justified because we are all citizens of the Occident, shaped by Catholicism, the Enlightenment, and the Reformation. One emergent feature of our current pluralism is the growth in numbers and public visibility of Catholics in a culture still riddled with anti-Catholic prejudice. Patterns of recent immigration are adding more Catholic citizens to our numbers. It behooves us to pay attention. We are dominantly a Protestant and not a Catholic nation. But mainline Protestantism, in recent decades, has so thoroughly embraced the expressivist-individualist pole of modernism that its spokesmen and spokeswomen find it increasingly difficult to address questions of community. Once again, what is at stake is not jettisoning a tradition—robust Protestant individualism—in favor of some other; rather, I have in mind to chasten the project of the untrammeled self with alternative readings of Christianity and civil society as traditions of discourse.

If one turns to recent Catholic social thought one finds, first, adamant criticism of "superdevelopment, which consists in an excessive amount of every kind of material good for the benefit of certain social groups." Superdevelopment "makes people slaves of 'possession' and of immediate gratification, with no other horizon than the multiplication of continual replacement of the things already owned with others still better. This is the so-called civilization of 'consumption' or 'consumerism,' which involves so much 'throwing away' and 'waste.' "[25]

The "sad effects of this blind submission to pure consumerism," argues Pope John Paul II, is a combination of materialism and a relentless dissatisfaction as "the more one possesses the more one wants." Aspirations that cut deeper, that speak to human dignity within a world of others, are stifled. John Paul's name for this alternative aspiration is "solidarity," not "a feeling of vague compassion or shallow distress at the misfortunes of so many people" but instead a determination to "commit oneself to the common good; that is to say, to the good of all and of each individual because we are really responsible for all." Through solidarity we *see* "the 'other' . . . not just as some kind of instrument . . . but as our 'neighbor,' a 'helper,'[26] to be made a sharer on a par with ourselves in the banquet of life to which we are all equally invited by God."[27] The structures that make possible this ideal of solidarity are the many associations of civil society "below" the level of the state.

To the extent that John Paul's words strike us as forbiddingly utopian or hopelessly naive, to that extent we have lost civil society. Or so, at least, Alan Wolfe concludes in his important book, *Whose Keeper? Social Science and Moral Obligation.* Wolfe updates Tocqueville, apprising us of how far we have come, or how rapidly we have traveled, down a road to more and more individualism requiring more and more centralization of political and economic power. For all our success in modern societies, especially in the United States, there is a sense, desperate in some cases, that all is not well, that something has gone terribly awry. We citizens of liberal democratic societies understand and cherish our freedom, but we are "confused when it comes to recognizing the social obligations that make . . . freedom possible in the first place."[28] This confusion permeates all levels, from the marketplace, to the home, to the academy.

The political fallout of our current moral crisis is reflected in the irony of a morally exhausted left embracing rather than challenging the logic of the market by endorsing the relentless translation of *wants* into *rights.* Although the left continues to argue for taming the market in a strictly economic sense, it follows the market model where social relations are concerned, seeing in any restriction of individual "freedom" to live any sort of lifestyle an unacceptable diminution of choice. On the other hand, many conservatives love the untrammeled (or the less trammeled the better) operations of the market in economic life but call for a restoration of traditional morality, including strict sexual scripts for men and women, in social life. Both rely either on the market or the state "to organize their codes of moral obligation" when what they really need is "civil society—families, communities, friendship networks, solidaristic workplace ties, voluntarism, spontaneous groups and movements— not to reject, but to complete the project of modernity."[29]

Wolfe reminds us that early theoreticians of liberal civil society were concerned to limit the sphere of capitalist economics by either assuming or reiterating a very different logic, the moral ties that bind in the realms of family, religion, voluntary association, community. The market model, Adam Smith insisted, should not be extended as a metaphor for a process of all-encompassing exchange. Were we to organize "all our social relations by the same logic we use in seeking a good bargain"—and this is the direction we are pushed by the individualist project—we could not "even have friends, for everyone else interferes with our ability to calculate conditions that will maximize self-interest."[30]

Nor is the welfare state as we know it a solution to the problems thrown up by the operations of the market. The welfare state emerged from a set of ethical concerns and passions which ushered in the conviction that the state was the "only agent capable of serving as a surrogate for the moral ties of civil society" as these began to succumb to market pressure. But over forty years of evidence is in, and it is clear that welfare statism as a totalizing logic erodes "the very social ties that make government possible in the first place." Government can strengthen moral obligations but cannot substitute for them. As our sense of particular, morally grounded responsibilities to an intergenerational web falters and the state moves in to treat the dislocations, it may temporarily "solve" delimited problems broadly defined; but these solutions, over time, may serve to further thin out the skein of obligation.

Just as Tocqueville did in the nineteenth century, Wolfe today appreciates that a social crisis is also an ethical crisis. Although he presents no menu of policy options, he calls for a "third perspective on moral agency different from those of the market and the state," one that "allows us to view moral obligation as a socially constructed practice negotiated between learning agents capable of growth on the one hand and change on the other."[31] This formulation is similar to one offered by David Hollenbach, S.J., when he endorses a "pluralist-analogical understanding of the common good and human rights." Hollenbach, with Wolfe, recognizes that social and institutional change is not only inevitable but needed "if all persons are to become active participants in the common good, politically, economically and culturally."[32]

At this point, Catholic social thought, here represented by Hollenbach, makes contact with American experiences and theories of community, association, local autonomy. Latter-day Tocquevillians and Catholic social thinkers share a hope—the hope that the social practices in which individuals engage in their everyday lives in modern American democracy are richer and reflect greater sociality than atomistic visions of the acquisitive, unencumbered self allow. Perhaps, they muse, most of us most of the time do *not* govern our lives by principles of exchange, despite the totalizing logic of rational-choice contractarians and hard-core individualists. The call is *not* for some utopian vision of participatory democracy but for a more effective, more authentic form of representative democracy embodied in genuinely viable, overlapping social institutions.

Framed by this horizon, the notion of rights central to the American tradition becomes the counterpart of responsibilities. Rights are not "spoken of primarily as individual claims. . . . Rights exist within and are relative to a historical and social context and are intelligible only in terms of the obligations of individuals to other persons."[33] This understanding of persons steers clear of the strong antinomies of individualism versus collectivism. Catholic social thought begins from a fundamentally different ontology from that assumed and required by individualism, on the one hand, and statism, on the other—assumptions that provide for *individuality* and rights as the goods of persons in community, together with the claims of social obligation. This version of individuality makes possible human unity as a cherished achievement and acts as a brake against coerced uniformity.

Or take these words from the U. S. Bishops' Pastoral Letter on the economy: "The dignity of the human person, realized in community with others, is the criterion against which all aspects of economic life must be measured." All economic decisions must be judged "in light of what they do *for* the poor, what they do *to* the poor and what they enable the poor to do *for* themselves."[34] The Bishops draw upon the principle of subsidiarity, central to Catholic social teaching, when they speak of the "need for vital contributions from different human associations," considering it a disturbance of the "right order" of things to assign to a greater and higher association what a "lesser" association might do. In this way, institutional pluralism is guaranteed and "space for freedom, initiative and creativity on the part of many social agents" is made possible.[35] Hollenbach calls this "justice-as-participation," noting that the Bishops' contribution to the current, deadlocked "liberal/communitarian debate" lies in the way justice is conceptualized "in terms of this link between personhood and the basic prerequisites of social participation."[36]

Summing up subsidiarity, Joseph A. Komonchak lists nine basic elements: (1) The priority of the person as origin and purpose of society; (2) The essential sociality of the human person, whose self-realization is through social relations—the principle of solidarity; (3) Social relationships and communities exist to provide help to individuals, and this "subsidiary" function of society does not supplant self-responsibility, but augments it; (4) "Higher" communities exist to perform the same subsidiary roles toward "lower" communities; (5) Communities must enable and encourage individuals to exercise their self-responsibility, and larger communities must do the same for smaller ones; (6) Subsidiarity serves as a principle to regulate interrelations between individuals and communities, and between smaller and larger communities; and (9) Subsidiarity is a universal principle, grounded in a particular ontology of the person.[37] Subsidiarity thus favors Tocqueville's associative version of democracy at its best and works to exclude unnecessary centralization. Subsidiarity is a theory of and for civil society that refuses stark alternatives between individualism and collectivism.

Ironically, or perhaps not so ironically, the richest theorizing of democratic civil society in the past decade or so has come from citizens of countries who were subjected for forty years or more to authoritarian, even totalitarian statist regimes. They pose positive alternatives to statism and individualism by urging that the associations of civil society be recognized as "subjects" in their own right. They want a genuinely pluralist law to recognize and sustain this associative principle as a way to overcome excessive privatization and excessive state control, as a way to achieve a diverse yet solidaristic democratic society.

Consider Solidarity theorist and activist Adam Michnik's characterization of democracy. In an interview, he insists that democracy

> entails a vision of tolerance, an understanding of the importance of cultural traditions, and the realization that cherished human values can conflict with each other. . . . The essence of democracy as I understand it is freedom—the freedom which belongs to citizens endowed with a conscience. So understood, freedom implies pluralism, which is essential because conflict is a constant factor within a democratic social order.

Michnik insists that the genuine democrat always struggles with and against his or her own tradition, eschewing thereby the hopelessly heroic and individualist notion of going it alone. Michnik here positions himself against our contemporary American tendency to see any defense of tradition as necessarily "conservative"; indeed, he criticizes our entire banalized and hopelessly rigid distinction between right and left. He proclaims: "A world devoid of tradition would be nonsensical and anarchic. The human world should be constructed from a permanent conflict between conservatism and contestation; if either is absent from a society, pluralism is destroyed."[38]

One final, vital voice, that of Vaclav Havel's. For years an oft-imprisoned champion of civic freedom and human rights, as well as Czechoslovakia's premier playwright, Havel is now, amazingly, the president of the Czech republic. In an essay on "Politics and Conscience," he writes:

> We must trust the voice of our conscience more than that of all abstract speculations and not invent other responsibilities than the one to which the voice calls us. We must not be ashamed that we are capable of love, friendship, solidarity, sympathy and tolerance, but just the opposite: we must see these fundamental dimensions of our humanity free from their "private" exile and accept them as the only genuine starting point of meaningful human community.

He adds:

> I favor "anti-political politics," that is, politics not as the technology of power and manipulation, of cybernetic rule over humans or as the art of the useful, but politics as one of the ways of seeking and achieving meaningful lives, of protecting them and serving them. I favor politics as practical morality, as service to the truth, as essentially human and humanly measured care for our fellow humans. It is, I presume, an approach which, in this world, is extremely impractical and difficult to apply in daily life. Still, I know no better alternative.[39]

Nor, in truth, do I.

At the conclusion of *Public Man, Private Woman,* I articulated a vision of an "ethical polity." I was not thinking specifically of diversity and unity, individuality and solidarity as I wrote, but that seems to have been what I was all along aiming for:

> Rather than an ideal of citizenship and civic virtue that features a citizenry grimly going about their collective duty, or an elite band of citizens in their public space cut off from a world that includes most of us, within the ethical polity the active citizen would be one who had affirmed as part of what it meant to be human a devotion to public, moral responsibilities and ends.

For the body is one but has many members.

NOTES

1. See, for example, Stephen Holmes's ill-tempered attack, "The Community Trap," *New Republic* 199 (November 1988): 24–29. Holmes charges the communitarians with reviling the tradition of freedom.

2. See Michael Walzer's analysis on p. 122.

3. Glenn Tinder, "Can We Be Good without God," *Atlantic* 264 (December 1989): 76.

4. David Hollenbach, S.J., "Liberalism, Communitarianism, and the Bishops' Pastoral Letter on the Economy," *Annual of the Society of Christian Ethics* (University of Tennessee), ed. D. M. Yeager (1987), p. 30.

5. See Ralph Ketcham, ed., *The Anti-Federalist Papers and the Constitutional Convention Debates* (New York: New American Library, 1986), p. 18.

6. Alexis de Tocqueville, *Democracy in America*, trans. Henry Reeve, rev. Francis Bowen, ed. Phillips Bradley (New York: Vintage Books, 1945), 2:293.

7. See Peter Brown, *The Body and Society: Men, Women, and Sexual Renunciation in Early Christianity* (New York: Columbia University Press, 1988). See also Peter Brown, *The Cult of the Saints* (Chicago: University of Chicago Press, 1981).

8. St. Augustine, *The City of God*, ed. David Knowles (Baltimore: Penguin Books, 1972), p. 876.

9. Tinder, "Can We Be Good," p. 72.

10. St. Augustine, *Confessions*, trans. R. S. Pine-Coffin (Baltimore: Penguin Books, 1961), pp. 199–200.

11. St. Augustine, *City of God*, p. 22.

12. Tinder, "Can We Be Good," p. 76.

13. See, for example, Margaret Miles, *Fullness of Life* (Philadelphia: Westminster Press, 1981); on bodily discipline and practices of the self see Michel Foucault, *The Use of Pleasure* (New York: Pantheon Books, 1985).

14. Hannah Arendt, *The Life of the Mind* (New York: Harcourt Brace Jovanovich, 1978), 2:88–89.

15. See Philip Abbott, *States of Perfect Freedom* (Amherst: University of Massachusetts Press, 1987).

16. This and the previous citation are from Elizabeth Cady Stanton's autobiography, *Eighty Years and More* (New York: Schocken Books, 1971), p. 231.

17. These and all later citations are drawn from Elizabeth Cady Stanton's speech, *The Solitude of Self* (Kailua, Hawaii: published privately by Doris M. Ladd and Jane Wilkins Pultz, 1979).

18. Sheldon Wolin, "Hannah Arendt: Democracy and the Political," *Salmagundi* (Spring–Summer 1983), p. 18.

19. Cited in Edward Abrahams, *The Lyrical Left* (Charlottesville: University of Virginia Press, 1986), p. 16.

20. Ibid., p. 17.

21. Ibid.

22. This quotation and those to follow on the World War I era are drawn from my book, *Women and War* (New York: Basic Books, 1987).

23. Quoted in Bruce Clayton, *Forgotten Prophet: The Life of Randolph Bourne* (Baton Rouge: Louisiana State University Press, 1984), pp. 189-90.

24. Randolph Bourne, *The Radical Will: Randolph Bourne, Selected Writings, 1911-1918*, ed. Olaf Hansen (New York: Urizen Books, 1977), p. 361.

25. Pope John Paul II, "Sollicitudo Rei Socialis," *Origins* 17 (March 1988): 650.

26. Cf. Gen. 2:18-20.

27. Pope John Paul II, "Sollicitudo Rei Socialis," pp. 654-55.

28. Alan Wolfe, *Whose Keeper? Social Science and Moral Obligation* (Berkeley: University of California Press, 1989), p. 2.

29. Ibid., p. 20.

30. Ibid., p. 30.

31. Ibid., p. 220.

32. David Hollenbach, "The Common Good Revisited," *Theological Studies* 50 (March 1989): 85.

33. Lisa Sowell Cahill, "Toward a Christian Theory of Human Rights," *Journal of Religious Ethics* 8 (Fall 1980): 284.

34. U.S. Catholic Bishops' Pastoral Message and Letter, "Economic Justice for All: Catholic Social Teaching and the U.S. Economy," *Origins* 16 (November 1986): 415.

35. Ibid., pp. 422-23.

36. Hollenbach, "Liberalism, Communitarianism, and the Pastoral Letter," p. 34.

37. Joseph A. Komonchak, "Subsidiarity in the Church: The State of the Question," *Jurist* 48 (1988): 301-20.

38. From an interview in *Times Literary Supplement* (February 19-25, 1968), pp. 188-89.

39. Vaclav Havel, *Living in Truth*, ed. Jan Vladislav (London: Faber and Faber, 1986), pp. 152, 155.

5

HOW TO MAKE A REPUBLIC WORK: THE ORIGINALITY OF THE COMMERCIAL REPUBLICANS

MICHAEL NOVAK

> Providence has been pleased to give this one connected country to one united people—a people descended from the same ancestors, speaking the same language, professing the same religion, attached to the same principles of government, very similar in their manners and customs, and who, by their joint counsels, arms, and efforts, fighting side by side throughout a long and bloody war, have nobly established their general liberty and independence.
>
> —John Jay, *Federalist* 2

Just over a hundred years ago, my family began the long voyage to the United States from the villages of Dubrava and Brutovce, high in the Tatra Mountains of Central Europe, near the birthplace of the written Slavic languages—and near the burial place of Attila the Hun. I have often had reason to breathe a quiet prayer of thanksgiving that they settled here rather than in the many other places to which Slovaks then emigrated. I am especially grateful that they settled in an Anglo-Saxon place, nourished in the traditions and habits of English common law and custom. Although I am a Roman Catholic, I am happy that they settled in a predominantly Protestant land, where religious life is deeply respected and religious liberty is a

I would like to thank the following researchers for their assistance, especially with the notes: Scott Walter (1987), David Foster (1989), and Kevin O'Halloran (1990). I also owe many challenges to my thinking about the Framers to two colleagues at the American Enterprise Institute (AEI), in particular, Robert Goldwin, head of an acclaimed series of studies on the Constitution, and Walter Berns, author of *Taking the Constitution Seriously*; and also to a former colleague at AEI, William A. Schambra. It should be noted that I do not write as a historian or political scientist but as a theologian concerned to understand the uniqueness (in Christian history) of the American experiment.

central impulse. I especially cherish the tradition of the "commercial republicans," a school of thought not solely but very largely Anglo-Saxon in its focus (even in Montesquieu). It is this tradition that I mean to highlight in our inquiry into diversity.

My aim is to stress the originality of the Founders, an originality of which they were poignantly conscious. This consisted chiefly in finding a practical solution to two key problems on which republican experiments had heretofore foundered: how to prevent the tyranny of a majority and how to defeat envy and divisiveness. Duly stressing both their originality and their practical wisdom, I want to highlight the plain, humble solution they offered, so often despised by those of aristocratic or moralistic bearing: that is, the lowly solution of encouraging commerce, industry, and invention. They did this to promote the energetic engagement of "the middling classes" in those prosaic tasks of economic growth that classical authors had looked down upon. In my youth, I did not appreciate the commercial, economic side of this brilliant solution; my teachers suggested that I should despise it. As so often happens in life, we look long and fruitlessly among faraway, high and mighty things, only to overlook the humble places where the secrets lie near at hand. What I like most about the commercial republicans is their willingness to take the lowly path, where the solution they were seeking had for centuries lain humbly buried.

ORIGINALITY AND PRACTICAL WISDOM

To build human life around practical wisdom is a distinctively Jewish and Christian impulse, a central thrust in what we mean by "the West." The God of Judaism and Christianity offers us in the Scripture the Names He most prefers: "I am Who am," Creator of all things, Truth, Light, Law. Not by accident does our Statue of Liberty bear in one upraised arm a light and, in the other, a book. Not by accident did Abraham Lincoln wholeheartedly support the Morrill Act, whose effect in 1862 was to base the development of the West upon the land-grant colleges and therefore upon practical, inventive intelligence, as the Homestead Act had based it upon the principle of free labor, which Lincoln judged to be prior to, and the superior of, capital.[1] The Framers of our Constitution knew—as Lincoln knew —that the cause of the wealth of nations is wit, discovery, invention, *caput* (L., the head). The defining element that distinguishes a capitalist from a traditional or mercantilist economy is neither private property nor markets nor profit (all of which are as traditional as biblical Jerusalem) but invention and discovery, as in the invention of Adam Smith's pin factory.

Jews and Christians are taught, in a way that Buddhists, Hindus, Animists, and others have not been taught, that it is our vocation not merely to reflect the world, to contemplate it, or to be reconciled with it (although all those things are both beautiful and necessary), but to change it: to probe it, to analyze it, to seek out its secrets, to reconstruct it, to complete it. Having been made in the image of the Creator, Jews and Christians believe, it is the vocation of humans to create. They are to build up and to prepare "the Kingdom of God." From this impulse toward inquiry came the great monasteries of the fourth century, the universities of the eleventh century, and eventually the great tide of invention and "progress" that so distinguishes the West.

Judaism and Christianity understand human nature as liberty and thus propel history with a cultural dynamism of which we are the heirs, and they root liberty in the pursuit of truth. Western universities and institutions of research have thus become history's cutting edge. In the U.S., in addition, an impulse toward diversity uncoils from our constitutional structure, which limits the state and empowers alternative centers of action. This twin impulse toward inquiry and diversity helps to explain why in the state of Ohio by the year 1872 there were already more colleges and universities than in all of France and Great Britain and how most of these came to be founded, not by the state, but by free associations of individuals, often Methodist, or Lutheran, or Catholic, or Episcopal, or Baptist, and so forth.

Three convictions, ancient in root but modern in their American form, lie behind this distinctive cultural dynamism: first, that human beings are made in the image of the Creator and fulfill their vocation by creating; second, that the cause of the wealth of nations is practical, inventive intellect, fashioned also in the image of God; third, that the free exercise of intellect and creativity requires institutions — an *ordo*, a *system* — worthy of the dignity with which human beings have been endowed by their Creator. (In the classical tradition, intellect has two sets of habits, theoretical and practical. Americans have clearly preferred the latter; but each feeds the other, and it would be wrong to think of Americans as merely practical). As Lord Acton describes it, "The History of Liberty" required centuries of reflection among Jews and Christians upon the identity that God had given them, before they could fashion institutions worthy of that endowment. Trial and error were required, experiments, partial steps, advances, and declines. And among the half-dozen greatest landmarks in that history was the Constitution of the United States.[2]

Lord Acton counted himself a follower of the "Whig tradition" and attributed to St. Thomas Aquinas "the earliest exposition of the Whig theory of revolution." Acton cites a passage written five centuries before the U.S. Declaration of Independence (about the same time that Simon de Montfort was summoning the English House of Commons) and suggests that it is from Thomas Aquinas, whose direct echo reverberates through the American Declaration:

> A king who is unfaithful to his duty forfeits his claim to obedience. It is not rebellion to depose him, for he is himself a rebel whom the nation has a right to put down. But it is better to abridge his power, that he may be unable to abuse it. For this purpose, the whole nation ought to have a share in governing itself; the constitution ought to combine a limited and elective monarchy, with an aristocracy of merit, and such an admixture of democracy as shall admit all classes to office, by popular election. No government has a right to levy taxes beyond the limit determined by the people. All political authority is derived from popular suffrage, and all laws must be made by the people or their representatives. There is no security for us as long as we depend on the will of another man.[3]

By 1776, "truths" more fully developed from such roots had come to seem to the American Founders as "self-evident" and a common heritage. In his splendid book on the U.S. Constitution, Walter Berns cites a claim of Thomas Jefferson that in America all Whigs "thought alike."[4] This claim suggests the essential cultural and philosophical unity of the Framers and the people whose consent they sought. Reference to the Whig frame of mind further suggests a respect for experience, for singulars, for contingents, for individuals, for habits, for traditions, for particularities—so to say, an Aristotelian rather than a Platonic approach to politics.

Although the Framers worked within a relatively homogeneous culture, the words they wrote down and the principles they enunciated embodied so much practical wisdom, distilled from experience, that in 200 years they have hardly had to be altered. To the contrary, one might argue that it has taken 200 years (and the process is not yet, is never, complete) for the habits and institutions of the nation slowly to live up to the full meaning of those original words.[5]

To repeat myself, I am eternally grateful that the U.S. Constitution was not framed in accord with the theories, habits, and traditions available in 1776 within Slavic cultures or Hispanic cultures, or African cultures, or Japanese, or French, or German, or any other cultures. When the Framers announced a *novus ordo seclorum* — an enormous claim, that: "the new order of the ages" — they were expressing their awareness of their own originality. There was no model they could follow. They were inventing a republic unlike any other, *sui generis*.[6] They were well-traveled men, among them some who had ransacked the libraries of Paris and London searching out precedents. Yet nowhere in the world of their acquaintance had they encountered any system like the one they chose to constitute. Forthrightly, they called theirs "new." A new world. A new *ordo*. A new republic. Even, a new Israel.

The Framers had, to be sure, learned much from Britain, whence they imbibed a sense of the common law, a tradition of individual liberty, an internalized sense both of common obligations and of personal individuality. But the Framers also knew themselves to be breaking away from the British model. And British writers knew it, too: not only Lord Acton a century later but also such writers as Adam Smith and Richard Cobden, who urged their countrymen to emulate the new experiments of the Americans, particularly in economics.[7]

What we are missing today, two hundred years after the Constitutional Convention, six score and two years after the death of Lincoln, is a sharp understanding of the originality of this American experiment. The Framers took it to be an experiment in accord with "the new science of politics."[8] Where in the university today, apart from a few specialists, would one find an understanding of that "new science of politics"? Where is the originality of these United States studied and emphasized? The Framers intended these principles to be universal. They thought themselves to be describing the "system of natural liberty," not solely the system of American liberty. They thought they were proceeding on behalf of all humankind. So also Lord Acton saw them. But do we so see them? Unless I am mistaken, the general intellectual mood is to derogate from the importance to other nations of this originality, even in some quarters to despise it and in others to ignore it.

Despite the wisdom that others see in our institutions, we ourselves have not been a philosophical people. I doubt if many Americans could write down an exact account of what the American experiment *is*. We live in considerable intellectual darkness about our Constitution's own first principles. The Chinese youngsters who carried a model of the Statue of Liberty in Shanghai in June, 1989, however, and the Eastern Europeans who in throwing out communism in the fall of 1989 so often cited American ideals do not ignore American originality. On the contrary, they hold it up as their model. The great French Catholic philosopher Jacques Maritain, one of the architects of the Universal Declaration of Human Rights of the United Nations, wrote of us: "You are advancing in the night, bearing torches toward which mankind would be glad to turn; but you leave them enveloped in the fog of a merely experiential approach and mere practical conceptualization, with no universal ideas to communicate. For lack of an adequate ideology, your lights cannot be seen."[9] Foreigners who would discover our secrets in their practical detail, American students who hunger to know their own national identity, and citizens in need of a standard by which to judge their progress have been left by and large without intellectual guides. In the academy more is known of Marx and socialism than of the distinctive principles of the American science of politics.

The blue-grey planet on which we live contains today 165 nations or so, 165 "orders" or "systems." Among these, indeed, there is diversity—but not in infinite range. And our uniqueness, too, is part of that diversity. It would be amiss to hunger after diversity abroad while neglecting the ways in which our own experiment is different from every other. Naturally, we should learn all we can about the others, be open to them, and raise questions endlessly. But to neglect our own distinctiveness would be to fail in what we alone can do: articulate before the world who and what we are.

HOW TO AVOID ENVY: THE AMERICAN SOLUTION

The American Framers were convinced of their originality and knew that they were undertaking a new experiment on behalf of all humankind. Moreover, they were painfully aware that the Constitutional Convention labored—from May until September 1787— under the watchful eye of Providence (imaged on the Great Seal of the United States), to Whom it bore weighty obligations on behalf of them (a more than Deist act) to pray for the intervention of Providence.[10]

The problem the Framers faced may be stated succinctly. Although all Americans believed in republican principles, republican experiments of the past had ended in bitter division, dissension, and self-destruction. The very idea of republican government had fallen into disrepute. According to the old science of politics, to succeed, republics had to be small, based upon friendship and upon respect for one another's virtue. Yet republican experiments had always failed, often speedily. Through careful reflection on past experience, the Framers diagnosed two main historical dangers to republics: from below, dissension arising out of envy and, from above, tyranny growing out of a dominant majority. They also believed that through a "new science of politics" they had discovered a practical solution to these problems, a solution the ancients and the medievals had had no way of knowing.

The first great problem was the problem of envy. To see how Madison solved this requires a larger discussion of the discovery of economics. The old science of politics had known little or nothing of economics. Lacking even the concept of "political economy," it had not grasped "the causes of the wealth of nations" and had rarely stooped to praise the humble utilitarian virtues of a republic built on commerce. Conceived in an aristocratic and (as it thought) nobler age, the old science of politics dismissed the moral ideal of commerce (if it thought of it at all) as an oxymoron. In the aristocracies of the past, the poverty and subservience of the many were taken for granted. No one took the poverty of the great majority to be a scandal, for no one knew a single case in which vast numbers of the poor had systematically risen out of poverty. Not until the late 1700s did the unprecedented success of the North American "colonies" provide such a case. The astounding evidence of this success, as Hannah Arendt notes,[11] awakened Europeans at last to the so-called "social problem" of the nineteenth century. If the American poor could in such large numbers rise from poverty, how could Europe justify the condition of its own *miserables?*

In the eighteenth century, European aristocrats had looked down upon the poor. They looked down, as well, upon persons of commerce, trade, and industry. They spoke a great deal about beauty, high manners, the love of things for their own sakes, and about virtue both personal and civic. Aristocrats prided themselves on the splendor of the circumstances of their daily living (their homes, their entertainments) and on heroic deeds of public service in peace and war. As Adam Smith pointed out, wealth in the early modern period typically lay in the inheritance of lands.[12] Roads and markets for the produce of these lands being few, the landed aristocracy had many incentives to consume their goods locally and so drew to themselves many retainers and maintained private armies. In such arrangements lay the cause of many quarrels, conflicts, and wars.

By the time of the Constitutional Convention of 1787 and the writing of *The Federalist*, however, original thinkers in France (Montesquieu) and Scotland (David Hume, Adam Ferguson, Adam Smith) had proposed a new social basis for a free society. Instead of relying upon the elevated sentiments of the nobility, they preferred the plain speech of the marketplace. Instead of relying upon a landed aristocracy, they thought the most solid foundation of a free society to be "the middling classes," that is, the many (of lowly birth) engaged in industry, trade, and commerce. While praising some aspects of the classic aristocratic virtues, they called attention also to their social costs, even absurdities. Instead of disdaining the merely useful activities of daily life, they celebrated those humdrum activities that actually improved the circumstances of ordinary people. Instead of rejecting commercial activities, they thought commerce indispensable to making free republics work—in the virtues it encouraged, in the opportunities it opened for the poor, and in the economic growth it spurred. Those who shaped this new and original school of thought came to be known, therefore as the "commercial republicans."

I have read no better account of the long, intellectual battle the commercial republicans fought than Ralph Lerner's chapter "Commerce and Character" in his collection *The Thinking Revolutionary*. And no writer better and more fully grasped what they accomplished, through their victory, than Alexis de Tocqueville in *Democracy in America*. This "band of brethren" included advocates as diverse as Montesquieu and John Adams, Adam Smith and Benjamin Franklin, David Hume and Benjamin Rush, who "were united at least in this: They saw in commercial republicanism a more sensible and realizable alternative to earlier notions of civic virtue and a more just alternative to the theological-political regime that had so long ruled Europe and its colonial periphery."[13] What did the commercial republicans oppose? Three things, chiefly: "visions of perfection beyond the reach of all or most; disdain for the common, useful, and mundane; judgments founded more on an individual's inherited status than on acts and demonstrated qualities."[14] In place of these, the commercial republicans promoted a twofold ideal: liberation from the inherited social order and liberation from old modes of ethical thinking. They dared to imagine "a new ordering of political, economic, and social life."[15]

A great part of the originality of the commercial republicans lay in their discovery of the principles of economics. By 1776 they had discovered, as Adam Smith put it in his title, the *Nature and Causes of the Wealth of Nations.* Henceforward, classic treatises "on politics" would have to be modified by the addition of the new term, "political *economy.*" Not by accident, many of Adam Smith's most penetrating empirical observations about what works for human prosperity and liberty— examples that he commended to Scotland and England for emulation —derived from experiments he had observed overseas in the North American "colonies." As if in reciprocation, the American Founders discovered in Adam Smith (and in his predecessors, especially Hume and Montesquieu) decisive encouragement. If they were, as Madison put it in *Federalist* 10, to rescue the republican idea "from the opprobrium under which it has so long laboured," they would have to make it work. Above all, they would have to keep it from that early dissolution into "faction and insurrection" into which all prior republics had so soon fallen. Here is where the new sophistication in economics was just what they needed.

So seriously did the authors of *The Federalist* take the threat from "faction and insurrection" that they devoted to it two whole numbers, 9 and 10. And they addressed the next two numbers, 11 and 12, to basic prerequisites of commerce. In the spirit in which Garry Wills writes in *Explaining America* of "The Hamiltonian Madison" and "The Madisonian Hamilton," all four numbers should be read together. Especially noteworthy in Number 12, to begin with, is Hamilton's praise of "the middling classes," whom Hume had already discerned as the best security of the free society: "The assiduous merchant, the laborious husbandman, the active mechanic, and the industrious manufacturer." This line marks a change of moral tone from the preference of the classical tradition for gentlemen and cavaliers. The whole of Hamilton's paragraph, in fact, celebrates this revolution in moral evaluation from aristocratic (agrarian) to commercial ideals:

> The prosperity of commerce is now perceived and acknowledged by all enlightened statesmen to be the most useful as well as the most productive source of national wealth, and has accordingly become a primary object of their political cares. By

multiplying the means of gratification, by promoting the introduction and circulation of the precious metals, those darling
objects of human avarice and enterprise, it serves to vivify and
invigorate all the channels of industry and to make them flow
with greater activity and copiousness. The assiduous merchant,
the laborious husbandman, the active mechanic, and the industrious manufacturer — all orders of men look forward with
eager expectation and growing alacrity to this pleasing reward
of their toils. The often-agitated question between agriculture
and commerce has from indubitable experience received a decision.[16]

Albert O. Hirschman has written brilliantly about this transformation in ideas, under the rubric of "The Arguments for Capitalism
Before its Triumph."[17] This transformation displaced the classic focus of politics, shifting it away from power and toward wealth. Regarding wealth, it showed that its classic source lay in plunder and
promoted instead invention and industry. Regarding morals, it
shifted from the classic, aristocratic view that the seeking of wealth
is "the root of all evil" to the new commercial republican view that
the moral pretensions of the aristocracy result in fact in the misery of
the poor. Compared to the seeking of power, glory, and honor by the
traditional aristocratic and warrior class, as Samuel Johnson put it,
"a man is seldom so innocently engaged, as in the getting of money."

To discourse further upon this pivotal argument of modern history would take us too far afield here. Suffice it to say that the authors of the Constitution and *The Federalist* came down decisively
on the side of the commercial republic: so decisively, that the paragraph from Hamilton quoted above, stressing the importance of
prosperity to the success of liberty, concludes as follows: "It is aston-
ishing that so simple a truth should ever have had an adversary; and
it is one, among a multitude of proofs, how apt a spirit of ill-
informed jealousy, or of too great abstraction and [aristocratic] refinement, is to lead men astray from the plainest truths of reason."

Hamilton, it is true, did not accept whole the theory of Montesquieu that a world of commercial republics would introduce final
peaceableness into history; he disputes this point at some length in
Federalist 6 and 7. Others of the commercial republicans also recognized that their new order would not come without costs. (Tocqueville was to count up these costs some forty years after the successful
ratification of the Constitution). Still, no less than Tocqueville, they
judged that the new American order would blaze a trail for all hu-

mankind. It would hitch the fate of the republican ideal to commerce — of democracy, as we say today, to capitalism. Not that the two cannot appear separately, the one without the other, as in history they sometimes briefly have, but rather that active commercial habits and the resulting economic growth are a necessary (but not sufficient) condition for the successful working of a republic. The Framers, of course, spoke of "acquiring" and "improving" property rather than, in the modern sense, of "economic growth." But there can be no doubt about their industriousness, their sense of great achievements waiting to be accomplished, and bustling, chance-taking energy. Of all this, Tocqueville gives admiring testimony.

For his part, Madison saw quite vividly in *Federalist* 10 that envy between social classes — between creditors and debtors, rich and poor — had helped destroy all earlier republics. Among social evils, envy is more destructive than hatred — more subtle, more easily rationalized, more easily disguised, and more corrosive. Envy destroys the instinct for the common good, setting part against part. How, then, to defeat envy? Only when every single part of the population has a well-grounded hope that each person or family can "improve its condition" does each focus its attention upon comparing its present lot with its future expectations. Otherwise, the normal tendency of humankind is to compare one's own present lot with the lot of others and to stand eager to pounce upon inequalities. For a stable republic, it is crucial that citizens compare their lot today with where, by hard work, effort, and luck, they expect to be tomorrow. This comparison of self with self across time offers a sense of self-mastery and achievement. It generates high morale. It evokes love for the Republic that makes it possible. The comparison of one's own lot with the lot of others, by contrast, breeds envy and generates what Madison called the "improper or wicked project" of equality.[18]

The chief cause of faction, Madison wrote, lies "in different degrees of acquiring property." The secondary cause lies in liberty. Nonetheless, to seek liberty is to have to cope with both property and faction. We will treat of property first and then of faction.

By property, Madison did not mean merely material things. On the contrary, he held that property "embraces everything to which a man may attach a value and have a right." This includes his life, faculties, and liberties, not only his material possessions. "As a man is said to have a right to his property, he may equally be said to have a property in his rights."[19] It would be a very grave intellectual error, then, to make the concept of property, so crucial to the history of liberty, merely materialistic in its scope, merely acquisitive in its modality, or merely a form of "possessive individualism." On the contrary, without the properties of life, liberty, and moral purpose, an individual would be stripped of all dignity whatever. And even in economic terms, the primary and most fecund form of wealth is intellectual property—ideas, inventions, new organizing concepts—rather than brute material things.

For the commercial republicans, a regime of private property is preeminently a social achievement. It is a basic social prerequisite for the exercise of human liberty. It is a crucial instrument of social justice (as the tradition of Catholic social thought has long recognized). A regime of private property gives ordinary citizens frequent and tangible reminders of the limits of state power.[20] In addition, it gives them the spiritual and material means of exercising their natural liberty in the physical public world, lest it remain entirely an "inner" freedom unable to be expressed in action. Third, a regime of private property, well protected over generations, gives industrious individuals many motives to labor intensively not solely for themselves but for future generations. By contrast, wherever private property is insecure, motives for personal industriousness are much diminished, prosperity declines, and envy more frequently rears its contorted face. The curtailment of private property is thus a grave depressant on economic prosperity and a source of much social conflict.

In brief, the solution of the commercial republicans to the perennial social destructiveness of envy was to promote economic vitality through commerce—and especially through an understanding of "improving" property that went far beyond the mere possession of material things. They thought of property as a dynamic principle, especially in the form of intellectual property and in the form of inalienable rights.

HOW TO AVOID FACTION AND INSURRECTION

In writing of the danger that faction and insurrection pose to the new republic, Madison is well prepared to propose a new vision of the public good. He takes care to describe the specific complaint which he is answering: "Complaints are everywhere heard from our most considerate and virtuous citizens . . . that the public good is disregarded in the conflicts of rival parties, and that measures are too often decided . . . by the superior force of an interested and overbearing majority."²¹ Two crucial points appear in this passage. First, Madison must find a way to achieve the public good. Second, he cannot locate the public good merely in the will of a majority, since the charge is that majorities ("interested" and "overbearing") already do prevail. These two points seem incompatible. If a majority cannot define the public good, who can?

Using materials he has learned from the commercial republicans, Madison advances an ingenious and novel solution (on which he later came to rest his hope of lasting fame). Factions cannot be eliminated. Neither can interests. The solution, then, is to control the effects of both.

Madison discerns two devices for doing this. First, rejecting the principle of the small republic ("small is safer"), he argued that the key to republican success lay in "the *enlargement* of the orbit"—that is, in a larger rather than a smaller size, in order to protect diversity. Classical philosophers had held that democracy is workable only in a small city (so that the voice of orators can be heard by all). Madison notes, by contrast, that small groups are easiest to stampede. Rhode Island or South Carolina or any other individual state may be easily tyrannized by its dominant interested majority. But the Union, reducing all these seeming local whales to smaller fish by its own much larger orbit, will be far safer against any local majority. The Union's diversity of climate, geography, and economic circumstance protects it from domination either by "a landed interest, a manufacturing interest, a mercantile interest, a moneyed interest," or by any "lesser interests."

By their very nature, commercial activities characteristically set interest against interest. Thus, the multiplication of commercial enterprises generates many rival factions. This great variety of factions and special interests works to secure the rights of minorities from the threat of dominant majorities. To this end, the promotion of rapid economic, commercial, and manufacturing growth is necessary for the preservation of republican principles. (To supply a recent example: The relative agrarian homogeneity of the South until after World War II inhibited the protection of the legal rights of Negroes.) Contrary to classical teaching, republican government is safer in a larger territory than in a smaller. Thus, the thirteen states united would form a republic safer than any one state alone.

The larger size of the American orbit, Madison first argued, would create room for many diverse interests, associations, and sects, preventing any one such from becoming a tyrannical majority that would trample on the rights of others. Not the small republic, but the large, would make for a "more perfect" union, since the larger orbit would make fundamental rights more secure. In the name of "the new science of politics," therefore, Madison argued for union rather than division, in order to increase the orbit. But his aim in doing so was to substitute *diversity* for *homogeneity*. In this respect, the national motto, *e pluribus unum*, has a particular and original force, almost the reverse of the one we usually think of, viz., that the many should flow into one. To the contrary, because of the Union there is diversity; without it, local tyrannies would be unchecked, as without the North southern slavery would have endured for decades longer.

Madison's second device for securing the public good is to make certain that the new, enlarged majority is thoroughly divided. Madison sees two causes of faction—liberty of opinion and diversity in the faculties of men. He notes that the talents and energies of free men regularly diverge, as do their opinions. "The diversity in the faculties of men, from which the rights of property originate, is . . . an insuperable obstacle to uniformity of interest." Then comes a very important sentence: "The protection of these faculties is the first object of government."[22] This is as if to say that the first duty of government is to protect inequality in property. Madison does not flinch from this hard truth. He follows his thought where it leads: "From that protection of different unequal faculties of acquiring property, the possession of different degrees and kinds of property immediately results; and from the influence of these on the sentiments and views of the respective proprietors, ensues a division of the society into different interests and parties."[23] Far from wringing his hands over such inequalities, at the end of Number 10 Madison describes "an equal division of property" as an "improper or wicked project."[24]

Madison is not dismayed by observing that "the latent causes of faction are thus sown in the nature of men; and we see them everywhere." He does not shrink from noting that human beings are "much more disposed to vex and oppress each other than to cooperate for the common good." The common good is, in fact, infrequently pursued. Worse, this "propensity of mankind to fall into mutual animosities" is so strong that, where no real reasons for friction exist, fanciful ones are invented. "But the most common and durable source of factions has been the various and unequal distribution of property." Not only is Madison not opposed to this inequality but also wishes by all practical means to increase the diversity of avenues to the acquiring of property and thus the kinds and types of inequality.

Madison returns to this point in *Federalist* 51: "If a majority be united by a common interest, the rights of the minority will be insecure. There are but two methods of providing against this evil." The first method would be "by creating a will in the community independent of the majority"— through "an hereditary or self-appointed authority." In other words, the authoritarian principle: The Maximum Leader who decides, "This is the common good. Follow me." Madison's judgment of this method is succinct: "This is, at best, precarious security." So he turns to his second method:

> The second method will be exemplified in the federal republic of the United States. Whilst all authority in it will be derived from and dependent on the society, the society itself will be broken into so many parts, interests and classes of citizens, that the rights of individuals, or of the minority, will be in little danger from interested combinations of the majority. In a free government the security for civil rights must be the same as that for religious rights. It consists in the one case in the multiplicity of interests, and in the other in the multiplicity of sects.[25]

(Pointedly, Madison leaves out a third way—exhorting and persuading the majority to seek the common good. Given what he has already argued, that would seem to be both utopian and foredoomed.) Clearly, Madison's aim is to multiply factions so that no one faction may accumulate a simple majority. Working majorities will always be necessary, but if their composition is diverse enough and ever changing, they can be formed only by a great deal of negotiation, after repeated attempts at mutual understanding. In this way, narrow viewpoints will give way to at least slightly larger ones, and the diverse factions will learn habits of mutual adjustment and cooperation. This enlargement of viewpoint may not go so far as to attain "the public good" *simpliciter*. But at least it should more closely approximate it than a hardened, inward-turning provincialism. Since property is the basic cause of faction, the key to preventing simple majorities is to promote a lively and diverse economic order. The key to such diversity is commerce.

Individual American citizens in an undiversified economy might easily fall into two large and simple classes, the rich and the poor, those who hold property and those who do not. That is the path that had already led to the collapse of so many republics in history. It

costs. Here Madison notes that not all economic interests are similar. A landed interest generates opinions and passions quite different from those of a mercantile interest. Capital-rich states differ from mineral-rich states. The highway interests differ from the canal interests. Overseas traders form opinions different from those of domestic manufacturers. This multiplicity of commercial and manufacturing activities can break up and check the traditional and prevalent agrarian interest, found in every state and dominant in some. Commerce is the one sure path to blocking the most likely social base for a "tyranny of the majority."

In addition, "the prosperity of commerce," which we have already seen Hamilton praise in Number 12, makes the channels of industry "flow with greater activity and copiousness." Citizens in large numbers see sustained improvement in the condition of their families. They set their own goals, less in contestation with others than in the pursuit of their own happiness, as each defines it. They are grateful to the system through which such abundant graces are shed upon them. They identify its advancement with further progress in improving their own condition. They lose their propensity to envy.

In short, often by allusive appeal to authors well known to their audience, Madison and Hamilton argue in *Federalist* 9 through 12 that union will afford greater security against faction and insurrection than disunion will and that the Union will be good for commerce, and commerce for the Union. Through a diversity as inherent in an enlarged Union as it is in commercial activities, the Union will much diminish the threat of the tyranny of the majority.

MORE ON THE COMMERCIAL REPUBLICANS

The influence of socialist arguments on historians since Vernon Parrington and Charles Beard has served to make many academics feel faintly ashamed of the nonsocialist tenor of the American Framers. This has led to such considerable neglect of the commercial republican tradition that it seems best, before concluding, to fill in the canvas a bit. Permit me to add a few colors in four specific areas. These touches do not constitute a full argument, I recognize; they are intended to arrest attention and focus it on something quite odd. Such concepts as private property and commerce, which have been so important to the success of the new American order and were so important to our Framers, seem an embarrassment to many contemporary academics. So strong a bias cannot be overcome quickly. Still, it contrasts sharply with the view of the commercial republicans that certain economic principles are a necessary (but not sufficient) condition for the success of republican self-governance. It seems useful to spell out at least five of the background principles on which the commercial republicans drew.

1. Ralph Lerner summarizes Montesquieu: " 'Commerce cures destructive prejudices'; it 'polishes and softens barbaric morals.' In making men more aware of both human variety and sameness, commerce made them less provincial and in a sense more humane. 'The spirit of commerce unites nations.' "[26] Montesquieu urged nations to devote themselves to commerce, and then "since their object was gain, not conquest, they would be 'pacific from principle.' " Lerner adds: "Even greater than these transnational benefits was the anticipated dividend in increased domestic security. . . . Relieved of the distortions imposed by ignorance and superstition, political life would come more and more to wear a human face." He quotes Hume: "Factions are then less inveterate, revolutions less tragical, authority less severe, seditions less frequent" and notes that "Smith seconded Hume's observation, pronouncing this effect the most important of all those stemming from commerce and manufacturing. Where before men had 'lived almost in a continual state of war with their neighbours, and of servile dependency upon their superiors,' now they increasingly had 'order and good government, and, with them, the liberty and security of individuals.' "[27]

Commercial activities, Madison had learned from Montesquieu, soften fanaticism, teach practical compromise, give instruction in prudence, temper manners, favor the works of peace, and attract ambitious men away from the allurements of war.

2. To focus the leading energies of a republic on material objects rather than on spiritual objects is more likely to prevent dissension, to nourish a spirit of compromise, and to make negotiation easier. Spiritual principles are indivisible and are not amenable to compromise. To make spiritual principles matters of central contention in a free republic is highly dangerous, because the glowing embers of the religious wars— not yet cold—might too easily be rekindled. By contrast, material things are divisible, deals may be struck, and negotiations may proceed on a reasonably calm basis. It is absolutely necessary, then, to give the citizens of a new republic many outlets for physical, material striving. Tocqueville was particularly impressed by this American characteristic and its importance for civic peace. (In our time, the debate over abortion may serve as an example of a divisive spiritual debate; how one side or the other may compromise

is not wholly clear, and there is little comfort to be gained, in such an issue, from the prospect of the tyranny of the one majority or the other.)

3. For Madison, the first task of government, and the first principle of justice, is to secure "the protection of different and unequal faculties of acquiring property."[28] This wholly virtuous and legitimate inequality is rooted in the normal diversity of individual natures, characters, and fortunes. That the American Proposition has this form of inequality as one of its necessary bases is clear enough. What is less often noted is that the American Proposition is designed to appeal solely to a people of cooperation and cannot appeal to a people given to envy. For its first principle holds that to protect inequality of certain kinds is essential for preserving liberty. It is important to see why this is so.

Private property is, in the most earthy of its several analogous senses, the material which the individual person fashions by his or her own insight and will. Private property is the instrument used in the pursuit of happiness. Human beings make quite different choices concerning property; through their distinctive use of it, they fashion the story of their lives. Absent rights to property, there is no material through which the free person might act in history. To respect individual liberty is therefore to respect different faculties for acquiring, disposing of, and using property.

In one respect, a regime of private property is a defense against uniformity and conformity. The greyness of regimes that have abolished it is legendary. In this sense, private property protects individuality. In another respect, however, the rationale for private property is the public good. No one holds that property rights are absolute. Their justification among commercial republicans is that through them humans best make improvements upon nature and thus enlarge the common patrimony of humankind.[29] No other regime in actual history except a regime of private property is more suited to advancing industriousness, imagination, invention, and social cooperation. This claim is an empirical one, found already in Aquinas.[30] Observing this regime in action in the United States, Crevecoeur had written:

> The American ought therefore to love this country much better than that wherein either he or his forefathers were born. Here the rewards of his industry follow with equal steps the progress of his labour; his labour is founded on the basis of nature, *self-interest*; can it want a stronger allurement? Wives and chil-

dren, who before in vain demanded of him a morsel of bread, now, fat and frolicsome, gladly help their father to clear those fields whence exuberant crops are to arise to feed and to clothe them all; without any part being claimed, either by a despotic prince, a rich abbot, or a mighty lord.[31]

4. Because of the influence of Marx, scholars too often assume that the essence of the commercial republic ("capitalism" is the name Marx gave to the economic system of "bourgeois democracy") consists in free markets, the private ownership of the means of production, and the accumulation of profits. These features, however, are wholly consistent with the precapitalist regimes of traditional mercantilism, such as Adam Smith was criticizing in Great Britain and other mercantile nations of 1776. Moreover, because of his own preoccupation with labor (and a particularly materialistic account of labor at that), Marx overlooked the key ingredient of a capitalist economy, whereas his American contemporary Abraham Lincoln did not.

The Americans were preoccupied with education rather than brute labor. The same Jefferson who prided himself coequally in the founding of the University of Virginia and the Declaration of Independence wrote to a young friend that he ought to read *The Wealth of Nations*, "the best book extant" on political economy.[32] And what struck the Americans in that book was its emphasis upon invention and discovery—as in the opening tale of the pin factory. Thus, Lincoln praised agricultural fairs as extraordinary instruments for the advancement of the rural economy, precisely because they diffused the new knowledge on which the production of wealth is based. Not only that, such fairs "stimulate that discovery and invention into extraordinary activity." In this, they fulfill the purposes of the patent-clause of the U.S. Constitution.[33] (The first and only time the word "right" is used in the body of the Constitution proper concerns the right, not to physical but to intellectual property, the right of "authors and inventors" to the fruit of their own inventions.) The cause of the wealth of nations is invention and discovery, not hard labor nor even an abundance of material property.

In the Homestead Act, Lincoln favored the diffusion of property holdings as widely as possible. In the Morrill Act, even in the midst of the Civil War, he secured the cause of the future wealth of the western states, the building of great universities in those then almost empty territories. He did this through the public provision of land-grant colleges to advance "the Progress of Science and useful Arts," according to the inspiration of Article I, section 8, clause 8, of the U.S. Constitution and according to his own words in his address to the Wisconsin State Fair of 1859. Later summarizing his own conception of the "proposition" to which the Union was committed, Lincoln expressed quite succinctly his understanding of "the principle of liberty":

> Without the *Constitution* and the Union, we could not have attained the result; but even these are not the primary cause of our great prosperity. There is something back of these, entwining itself more closely about the human heart. That something is the principle of "Liberty to all"—the principle that clears the path for all—gives *hope* to all—and by consequence, *enterprise* and *industry* to all.[34]

"The great difference between Young America" and old Europe, Lincoln said in a truly brilliant speech on 11 February 1859, "is the result of *Discoveries, Inventions,* and *Improvements.* These, in turn, are the result of *observation, reflection,* and *experiment.*"[35] Lincoln uses as an example how many hundreds of thousands of men must have watched "the fluttering motion" of an iron lid on a pot of boiling water before one of them thought to make an experiment to harness steam power. He praises the great inventions of history that have facilitated "all other inventions and discoveries," and singles out four of them: the invention of writing; the invention of printing; the discovery of America (and thus the emancipation of thought and the propensity of new frontiers to advance civilization and the arts); and the introduction of the patent laws. On the last point, because it has all the marks of the commercial republican point of view, joining Lincoln's thought to Madison's, let me quote in full:

> Next came the Patent laws. These began in England in 1624; and, in this country, with the adoption of our constitution. Before then, any man might instantly use what another had invented; so that the inventor had no special advantage from his own invention. The patent system changed this; secured to the inventor, for a limited time, the exclusive use of his invention; and thereby added the fuel of interest to the fire of genius, in the discovery and production of new and useful things.[36]

5. Finally, I would like to note that, whereas many of our contemporaries think of commerce in terms of laissez-faire, individualism, the cash nexus, and as opposite to communitarianism, for the Fram-

ers and for their intellectual forebears (such as Hume and Smith) commerce represented a new and superior way of building community. Recalling the relative isolation of the precapitalist agrarian life, these thinkers held that commerce would bring widely dispersed villages into bustling, informative, self-enlarging, voluntary, creative, pacific, and lawlike association. Tocqueville is particularly good on the question of why democracies tend toward commerce and industry and why commercial and industrial societies tend toward democracy but above all on the excitement, romance, and chanciness of commerce. He has his reservations about commerce (although among aristocrats he is astonishingly favorable to it), but these are not nearly so great as his reservations about the alternatives. In brief, it is important to see the extent to which the Framers were communitarians even in putting so much faith in commerce and the new possibilities opened up by contemporary economics. Their example teaches us, at the very least, not to use the word "community" in too uncritical, nostalgic, and premodern a sense.

CONCLUSION

The Framers, like Lincoln, had every reason to support an enlarged Union—an *unum*—in order to secure the inalienable rights cherished by a republican people. But they also had every reason to support a principle of pluralism—*e pluribus*—in order to make that Union safe from both a tyrannical majority and an envious mob. Their originality lay as much in their new principles for the new nation's economy as in their principles for its polity. Indeed, for reasons of this two-sided originality, the name they have been given combines both sets of principles, "commercial" and "republican." Better than their critics, they saw that by such principles as they had learned from their "new science of politics," they would secure a longer lasting love for the public good, a more enduring spirit of cooperation and voluntary association, and a greater love for constitutional unity than any republic has ever yet achieved.

In our very variety, we in the United States still remain, two hundred years later, one brotherly and sisterly people. Protecting "private rights," we enjoy an unprecedented degree of "public happiness." Our diversity protects our unity. Permit me to close with the plea James Madison addressed to the nation in *Federalist* 14, in the perilous days during which the Constitution lay in danger of failing ratification:

I submit to you, my fellow-citizens, these considerations, in full confidence that the good sense which has so often marked your decisions will allow them their due weight and effect; and that you will never suffer difficulties, however formidable in appearance or however fashionable the error on which they may be founded, to drive you into the gloomy and perilous scene into which the advocates for disunion would conduct you. Hearken not to the unnatural voice which tells you that the people of America, knit together as they are by so many cords of affection, can no longer live together as members of the same family; can no longer continue the mutual guardians of their mutual happiness; can no longer be fellow-citizens of one great, respectable, and flourishing empire.

We can imagine Madison looking up from his desk for a moment before again setting quill to paper:

Hearken not to the voice which petulantly tells you that the form of government recommended for your adoption is a novelty in the political world; that it has never yet had a place in the theories of the wildest projectors; that it rashly attempts what it is impossible to accomplish. No, my countrymen, shut your ears against this unhallowed language. Shut your hearts against the poison which it conveys; the kindred blood which flows in the veins of American citizens, the mingled blood which they have shed in defense of their sacred rights, consecrate their Union and excite horror at the idea of their becoming aliens, rivals, enemies.

Madison was eager to protect his own—and the Constitutional Convention's—originality, lest his fellow citizens overlook it:

Is it not the glory of the people of America that, whilst they have paid a decent regard to the opinions of former times and other nations, they have not suffered a blind veneration for antiquity, for custom, or for names, to overrule the suggestions of their own good sense, the knowledge of their own situation, and the lessons of their own experience? To this manly spirit posterity will be indebted for the possession, and the world for the example, of the numerous innovations displayed on the American theater in favor of private rights and public happiness.

The diminutive Madison, all of five-foot-six, wanted no one to overlook the creation of a *novus ordo* never seen on earth before, yet of enormous significance for the entire human race:

> Had no important step been taken by the leaders of the Revolution for which a precedent could not be discovered, no government established of which an exact model did not present itself, the people of the United States might at this moment have been numbered among the melancholy victims of misguided councils, must at best have been laboring under the weight of some of those forms which have crushed the liberties of the rest of mankind. Happily for America, happily we trust for the whole human race, they pursued a new and more noble course. They accomplished a revolution which has no parallel in the annals of human society. They reared the fabrics of governments which have no model on the face of the globe.

Thus was fashioned "a new order of the ages." The American Catholic bishops meeting in the Third Plenary Council of Baltimore in 1884, well formed in the "old science of politics" and the classic Catholic conception of order, had good cause to be grateful to the Framers. The bishops recognized both the novelty of the Framers and the Providence whence it sprang. They formally declared of the Framers that they built "wiser than they knew."[37] Along with Jews and all the diverse Protestants, Catholics were allowed through the "new science of politics" to feel at home here, and quite beyond toleration, invited into full and equal participation. *E pluribus unum.*

NOTES

1. Lincoln held "that labor is prior to, and independent of, capital; that, in fact, capital is the fruit of labor, and could never have existed if labor had not first existed — that labor can exist without capital, but that capital could never have existed without labor . . . that labor is the superior — greatly the superior — of capital." "Address before the Wisconsin State Agricultural Society, Milwaukee, Wisconsin," 30 September 1859, in Roy P. Basler, ed., *The Collected Works of Abraham Lincoln*, 8 vols. (New Brunswick, N.J.: Rutgers University Press, 1953), 3:478 (emphasis in original).

2. Of the U.S. Constitution, Acton wrote, "the powers of the states were actually enumerated, and thus the states and the union were a check on each other. That principle of division was the most efficacious restraint on democracy that has been devised." He added: "By the development of the

principle of Federalism, it has produced a community more powerful, more prosperous, more intelligent, and more free than any other which the world has seen." Lord Acton, *Lectures on Modern History*, intro. Hugh Trevor-Roper (New York: Meridian Books, 1961), chap. 19, "The American Revolution," p. 295.

3. As quoted in "The History of Freedom in Christianity," in Lord Acton, *Essays on Freedom and Power*, ed. Gertrude Himmelfarb (Cleveland, Ohio: World Publishing Co., 1955), p. 88.

4. Jefferson wrote a friend, "With respect to our rights, and the acts of the British government contravening those rights, there was but one opinion on this side of the water. All American Whigs thought alike on these subjects." The Declaration of Independence, continued Jefferson, neither aimed "at originality of principle or sentiment, nor yet copied from any particular and previous writing, . . . [it] was intended to be an expression of the American mind, and to give to that expression the proper tone and spirit called for by the occasion. All its authority rests then on the harmonizing of the sentiments of the day, whether expressed in conversation, in letters, printed essays, or in the elementary books of public right, as Aristotle, Cicero, Locke, Sidney, etc." Thomas Jefferson to Henry Lee, 8 May 1825, in Adrienne Koch and William Peden, eds., *The Life and Selected Writings of Thomas Jefferson* (New York: Modern Library, 1944), p. 719; quoted in Walter Berns, *Taking the Constitution Seriously* (New York: Simon and Schuster, 1987), p. 251.

5. Cf. Walter Berns: "Slavery was abolished by constitutional amendment, but, to do that, no one word of the preexisting text had to be amended or deleted.

Constitutional amendments were required to remove state barriers to black and female suffrage, but not a word of the Constitution had to be changed to *allow* blacks and women to vote.

Women now serve in House and Senate, on the Supreme Court, and will, almost surely, soon be elected vice president and eventually president, but to accomplish this not one word of the Constitution had or will have to be changed.

No constitutional change was required to allow 'Jews, Turks, and infidels' to vote or hold political office." Berns, *Taking the Constitution Seriously*, pp. 238–39.

6. Marvin Meyers argues that "although Hume's essay, 'Idea of a Perfect Commonwealth,' might have suggested to Madison some advantages of a large republic, it does not touch the crucial Madisonian argument from the number and diversity of social-economic interests. Montesquieu's famous defense of confederate government includes an argument for controlling the violence of faction that Madison adopted; but it is not the fundamental argument of *Federalist* 10. See *The Spirit of the Laws* 1: bk. 9, sec. 1. One could even look back to Aristotle, who proposes that large political societies have a large 'middle class,' citizens of moderate property who sustain a

moderate constitution; yet this is so, he argues, because such states are generally more free from factions of rich and poor, which is not exactly Madison's point. See *Politics*, bk. 4, chap. 11, sec. 13." "Beyond the Sum of the Differences: An Introduction," *The Mind of the Founder: Sources of the Political Thought of James Madison*, ed. M. Meyers (Indianapolis: Bobbs-Merrill, 1973), p. xxix, n. 8.

7. Adam Smith wrote: "There are no colonies of which the progress has been more rapid than that of the English in North America.

Plenty of good land, and liberty to manage their own affairs their own way seem to be the two great causes of the prosperity of all new colonies.

In the plenty of good land the English colonies of North America, though, no doubt, very abundantly provided, are, however, inferior to those of the Spaniards and Portugueze, and not superior to some of those possessed by the French before the late war. But the political institutions of the English colonies have been more favourable to the improvement and cultivation of this land, than those of any of the other three nations." Adam Smith, *An Inquiry into the Nature and Causes of the Wealth of Nations*, ed. R. H. Campbell, A. S. Skinner, and W. B. Todd, 2 vols. (Oxford: Clarendon Press, 1976, and Indianapolis: Liberty Classics, 1981), 2:571–72. In his first political essay, Richard Cobden wrote: "It is to the industry, the economy, and peaceful policy of America, and not to the growth of Russia, that our statesmen and politicians, of whatever creed, ought to direct their anxious study; for it is by these, and not by the efforts of barbarian force, that the power and greatness of England are in danger of being superseded." "England, Ireland, and America," in Francis W. Hirst, ed., *Free Trade and Other Fundamental Doctrines of the Manchester School* (1903; reprint ed., New York: Augustus M. Kelley, 1968), p. 73.

8. In the ninth *Federalist*, Madison went so far as to say that earlier republics had been "disordered" and "if it had been found impracticable to have devised models of a more perfect structure, the enlightened friends to liberty would have been obliged to abandon the cause of that species of government as indefensible. The science of politics, however, like most other sciences, has received great improvement. The efficacy of various principles is now well understood, which were either not known at all, or imperfectly known to the ancients. The regular distribution of power into distinct departments; the introduction of legislative balances and checks; the institution of courts composed of judges holding their offices during good behavior; the representation of the people in the legislature by deputies of their own election: these are wholly new discoveries, or have made their principal progress towards perfection in modern times. They are means, and powerful means, by which the excellencies of republican government may be retained and its imperfections lessened or avoided. To this catalogue . . . I shall venture . . . to add one more, on a principle which has been made the foundation of an objection to the new Constitution; I

mean the ENLARGEMENT of the ORBIT within which such systems are to revolve."

9. Jacques Maritain, *Reflections on America* (New York: Charles Scribner's Sons, 1958), p. 188. Maritain added: "The vital, pragmatic, completely unsystematic pressure exercised by the American people and the American soul on the structures of our modern industrial civilization is transforming from within the inner dynamism and historical trends of the industrial regime. It is causing this regime to pass beyond capitalism. The people have thus vanquished the inner logic of the industrial regime considered in its first historical phase, and have, almost without knowing it, inaugurated a really new phase in modern civilization." Ibid., p. 23.

10. The Constitutional Convention was seriously divided over the question of whether representation in Congress should be equal for all states or proportionate to each state's population. James Madison gave a speech pleading for a compromise, after which Franklin called for daily "prayers imploring the assistance of Heaven." The next day, 29 June, William Johnson of Connecticut proposed the terms from which the compromise emerged two weeks later. Berns, *Taking the Constitution Seriously*, pp. 101, 106.

11. Hannah Arendt, *On Revolution* (New York: Viking Press, 1965), p. 15.

12. See *An Inquiry into the Nature and Causes of the Wealth of Nations*, ed. R. H. Campbell et al. (Indianapolis: Liberty Classics, 1976), 1: bk. 3, chap. 3, "Of The Discouragement of Agriculture in the antient State of Europe after the Fall of the Roman Empire."

13. Ralph Lerner, *The Thinking Revolutionary: Principle and Practice in the New Republic* (Ithaca, N.Y.: Cornell University Press, 1987), p. 195.

14. Ibid., p. 196.

15. Ibid.

16. *Federalist* 12. For the passages in Wills, see *Explaining America* (New York: Doubleday, 1981), sects. 1 and 2, especially chap. 8.

17. Albert O. Hirschman, *The Passions and the Interests: Political Arguments for Capitalism before its Triumph* (Princeton, N.J.: Princeton University Press, 1977).

18. Madison feared "a rage for paper money, for an abolition of debts, for an equal division of property, or for any other improper or wicked project." He criticized "theoretic politicians" who "erroneously supposed that by reducing mankind to a perfect equality in their political rights, they would at the same time be perfectly equalized in their possessions, their opinions, and their passions." *Federalist* 10.

19. James Madison, "Property," *National Gazette*, 27 March 1792, in *Letters and Other Writings of James Madison* (Philadelphia: Lippincott, 1884) 4: 478. Quoted in Berns, *Taking the Constitution Seriously*, pp. 178–79.

20. "A right to property—a parcel of land, a house, a room of one's own,

or whatever—is a tangible reminder (and for most of us, the most effective reminder) of other rights and, therefore, of the proper limits of government." Berns, *Taking the Constitution Seriously*, p. 179.

21. *Federalist* 10.

22. Ibid.

23. Ibid.

24. Ibid.

25. *Federalist* 51.

26. Lerner, "Commerce and Character," in *Thinking Revolutionary*, p. 207, quoting Montesquieu, *L'esprit des lois*, bk. 20, sects. 1, 2, 7, 8.

27. Lerner, *Thinking Revolutionary*, pp. 208–9, quoting David Hume, "Of Refinement in the Arts," in *Essays*, pp. 280–81 and 283–84; and Adam Smith, *Wealth of Nations*, bk. 3, chap. 4.

28. *Federalist* 10.

29. Locke argued that "he who appropriates land to himself by his labor does not lessen but increase the common stock of mankind; for the provisions serving to the support of human life produced by one acre of enclosed and cultivated land are—to speak much within compass—ten times more than those which are yielded by an acre of land of an equal richness lying waste in common. And therefore he that encloses land, and has a greater plenty of the conveniences of life from ten acres than he could have from a hundred left to nature, may truly be said to give ninety acres to mankind." *Second Treatise of Government*, ed. Thomas P. Reardon (New York: Macmillan, 1986), par. 37. In section 43, Locke adds that the ratio is probably not ten to one but a thousand or more to one.

John Stuart Mill defended property on roughly the same grounds: "Whenever, in any country, the proprietor, generally speaking, ceases to be the improver, political economy has nothing to say in defense of private property, as there established." He adds that "no man made the land. It is the original inheritance of the whole species. Its appropriation is wholly a question of general expediency. When private property in land is not expedient, it is unjust. . . . Even in the case of cultivated land, a man whom, though only one among millions, the law permits to hold thousands of acres as his single share, is not entitled to think that all this is given to him to use and abuse, and deal with as if it concerned nobody but himself. . . . In everything which he does with [the land], and in everything which he abstains from doing, he is morally bound, and should, whenever the case admits, be legally compelled to make his interest and pleasure consistent with the public good." Mill, *Principles of Political Economy*, ed. Sir William Ashley (1909; reprint ed., New York: Augustus M. Kelley, 1969), pp. 231, 233–35.

30. Pope John Paul II makes this argument in *Laborem Exercens*, 15: "The person who works desires not only due remuneration for his work; he also wishes that within the production process provision be made for him to be able to know that in his work, even on something that is owned in com-

mon, he is working 'for himself.' This awareness is extinguished within him in a system of excessive bureaucratic centralization, which makes the worker feel that he is just a cog in a huge machine moved from above. . . . In the mind of St. Thomas Aquinas, this is the principal reason in favor of private ownership of the means of production."

31. J. Hector St. John Crevecoeur, *Letters from an American Farmer* (1782; reprint ed., New York: Fox, Duffield, 1904), p. 55.

32. Jefferson advised a friend beginning the study of law to read Smith's *Wealth of Nations*, "the best book extant" in political economy. Thomas Jefferson to Thomas Mann Randolph, 30 May 1790, in Koch and Peden, *The Life and Selected Writings of Thomas Jefferson*, p. 496.

33. Lincoln explained why he was proud to be asked to address an agricultural fair: "The chief use of agricultural fairs is . . . to make mutual exchange of agricultural discovery, information, and knowledge; so that, at the end, *all* may know every thing, which may have been known to but *one*, or to but a *few*, at the beginning—to bring together especially all which is supposed to not be generally known, because of recent discovery, or invention.

And not only to bring together, and to impart all which has been *accidentally* discovered or invented upon ordinary motive; but, by exciting emulation, for premiums, and for the pride and honor of success—of triumph, in some sort—to stimulate that discovery and invention into extraordinary activity. In this, these Fairs are kindred to the patent clause of the Constitution of the United States; and to the department, and practical system, based upon that clause." "Address before the Wisconsin State Agricultural Society, Milwaukee, Wisconsin," 30 September 1859, in *Collected Works of Abraham Lincoln*, 3:472 (emphasis in original).

34. "Fragment on the Constitution and the Union," January 1861, ibid., 4:168–69.

35. Abraham Lincoln, *Abraham Lincoln: Speeches and Writings 1859–1865*, ed. Don E. Fehrenbacher (New York: Library of America, 1989), pp. 4ff.

36. Ibid., pp. 10–11.

37. Third Plenary Council of Baltimore, "Pastoral Letter (1884)," in Hugh J. Nolan, ed., *Pastoral Letters of the American Hierarchy, 1792–1970*, 4 vols. (Huntington, Ind.: Our Sunday Visitor, 1971), 1:177.

6

CONSTITUTIONAL RIGHTS AND THE SHAPE OF CIVIL SOCIETY

MICHAEL WALZER

I

The Constitution of the United States is really two separate documents, two texts, written at different times, for different purposes, at the behest of different people. The first text is the original unamended seven articles, the Constitution itself; the second text is the Bill of Rights, the first ten amendments plus those parts of the original and of subsequent amendments that are now read in terms of rights theory. The two are dissimilar in style, opposite to one another as political programs, and intimately joined in practice.

The first text provides a design for state and government. Its purpose is to create a strong and centralized regime restrained by a set of internal, institutional checks and balances. The political machinery is meant to be powerful; the restraints are built in, part of the machine and not dependent on the good will or political intelligence of the operators of the machine. The Founders did not have much faith in anyone's good will, though they were, it has to be said, fairly confident at least about their own political intelligence. That confidence doesn't seem today to have been mistaken. The machinery they designed has no doubt been used in ways they did not foresee and would not have approved, but it is, two hundred years later, almost entirely in place. Current proposals for changing it (the six-year presidential term, for example) are of the tinkering sort, a trib-

After reading this paper at DePauw University, I also read it at Hebrew University in Jerusalem and at the University of Bologna. I am grateful to all those who listened and argued. Sanford Levinson read an early draft, and his incisive questions and criticisms helped greatly in the process of revision.

ute to the enduring value of what is being tinkered with. That is not to say, obviously, that the Constitution makes it impossible for political leaders to behave stupidly or immorally. But it does make it unlikely that a leader behaving in such a way won't encounter institutional opposition. Somewhere in the state machine, officials will find it in their personal interest, or in the interest of their offices, to scrutinize, criticize, resist, and counteract the policies of the leader. He will then complain that something is wrong with the machine; he can't make it run. But that's what the machine is like; that's when it is running according to its constitutional design.

If the first text is focused on the state, the second text is focused on civil society. It is in part the work of men who were worried by the state machine and who were critical of the specific design of the Founders. The second text opposes the first: Its most passionate advocates had little confidence in the internal checks and balances; they insisted instead on a set of external restraints, a statement of principles, a "bill" of rights.[1] The Bill is meant to fix the boundaries of future state action: All that is most valued in civil society lies on the other side, off limits. Churches, political assemblies, newspapers, private homes, and finally individual men and women are protected against political interventions. (The separate states are also protected, but I shall not focus on them just now.)

By and large the external restraints have held or, at least, they have been restored after each partial collapse; they have never collapsed entirely. This is so only because they were incorporated into the machine itself, admitted to a central role in the regime of checks and balances. The Supreme Court has made the Bill of Rights its own bill of entitlement and has undertaken actively to enforce what would otherwise be a merely hortatory document. It is not the case that the Court's claim to "judicial review" hangs on the Bill; it was first asserted on the basis of what appears to be an unproblematic account of judicial jurisdiction, part of the original Constitution. Yet the claim would be far less significant without the second text. Despite *Marbury* v. *Madison*, the Court is likely to have remained, without the second text, the weakest, "the least dangerous," of the three branches of government.[2] Ironically, the Court has been strengthened not only with regard to the president and the Congress but also with regard to civil society itself. What the state machine protects it can also subvert. The greater the power to protect, the greater the power to subvert.

It is hard now to imagine what the first text would be like without the second, the Constitution without the Bill of Rights (or with the

Bill only as a hortatory addendum). The political machine would certainly be different, and so might the society be that it organizes and protects. But perhaps that society, even as it was at the end of the eighteenth century, required the Bill; required just this inscription of rights; wrote, so to speak, its own ticket. We have a Bill of Rights because we have a diverse and pluralistic society. It's not that the Bill is functional to the society but rather that it expresses the sensitivities and aspirations of the members. Whether it is actually helpful to them, either as individuals or as a "people," is precisely what is at issue in many constitutional debates. The sensitivities and aspirations are not at issue. American civil society has its origin in acts of resistance to and flight from religious persecution. The primary purpose of the Bill of Rights is to make such persecution and all its well-remembered political and judicial concomitants impossible. Rights are entitlements to nonconformity and dissidence. The first ten amendments are acts of self-defense on the part of potential nonconformists and dissidents, collective efforts to guarantee diversity; and one may assume that a society capable of such efforts early on would have been capable of them later, too. Still, the textual guarantees are impressive and valuable.

So the Supreme Court became the guardian not of platonic virtue but, in the first instance at least, of Protestant conscience. And given what it means to be conscientious, the justices did not have to convince themselves that particular consciences were virtuous or necessarily right in their protestations in order to conclude that they were worth guarding. Conscience had only to be sincere. Understood in this way, the right of conscience was simply another name for the freedom of the individual. The aura of conscience extended to the whole person, to the mind and spirit that conscience guides, the physical body in which it lives, the home where it is nourished, the activities it inspires. All these are protected as the concentric circles around a sacred center—the individual who shares knowledge (co-science) with God. As the ancient Jews built walls around their Torah, protecting one law with another, so the Americans built walls around the individual, protecting one right with another. The Court guards the walls.

It is commonly said that property is the original right, the right that lies at the heart of the liberal enterprise.[3] Original it probably is so far as early modern legal history goes, but I have come to believe, reading the political and religious literature of the seventeenth and eighteenth centuries, that conscience is theoretically central from the beginning. What makes Lockean self-ownership plausible is the moral self-possession of Protestant men and women, who know, better than anyone else, how they ought to live. They also know, better than anyone else, how they should invest their labor and how they should use the products of their labor. Perhaps these two sorts of knowledge are ideologically as well as theoretically related. I have no reason to deny that the long list of rights reflects economic as well as religious interests. The aura, however, as one might expect, comes from religion, and that is not unimportant. If it serves to strengthen the moral and political claims of property, it also makes it impossible to focus exclusively on those claims. Property belongs to some, conscience to all; property is oligarchic, conscience democratic (or anarchic); given our history, however, the one will always call the other to mind.

The "unencumbered self" of liberal doctrine, so evocatively described by Michael Sandel, bears in its original form the encumbrances of divinity; and it derives from those encumbrances the larger part of its attraction.[4] The individual is bound to his God — the singular possessive pronoun is very important — and unencumbered only with reference to his fellow men. "Whatsoever hopes or obligations I should be bound with," an English radical of the 1640s told Oliver Cromwell, "if afterwards God should reveal himself, I would break it speedily, if it were an hundred a day."[5] It is because of his close and personal relation to God that someone like that is capable of "protestantism" in every other relation. The list of obligations and impositions against which conscientious men and women have protested is very long: church attendance, religious oaths, military conscription, censorship, tithes and taxes, expropriation and eminent domain, public health laws, paternalistic regulation, marriage vows, and so on. Some of these protests are successful, others are not; some of them may be divinely authorized, others, we can safely assume, are not; they are all made possible by the existence of an individual putatively tied to God and then constitutionally authorized to have scruples about every other tie.

This authorization is conservative in its consequences insofar as the Bill of Rights reflects the actually existing civil society and insofar as individuals are already possessed of their rights: holding in their hands whatever it is they take to be rightfully theirs, free in fact from all the bonds that they regard as illegitimate. In theoretical terms, the Constitution turns the privileged position of such individuals into a matter of law; in practical terms, it fortifies positions that might otherwise be radically exposed to the assaults of democratic majorities (although these assaults have turned out to be less dangerous than expected). The case is clearest with regard to property owners, where a rights-oriented interpretation of the due process clause made possession, unless it came by way of force or fraud, into a legal and moral entitlement that was effective for decades against strongly based reform movements. But there are other examples. Consider the extraordinary longevity of the original assignment of conscientious objector status (by most of the thirteen states) to the enrolled members of certain explicitly named Protestant sects. Today's members possess those rights as a virtual inheritance, and because of this possession it has been difficult to claim the same or similar rights for anyone else. If for much of its history the Supreme Court was the defender of the economic status quo, it was also, though more intermittently, the defender of the religious status quo. And the same defense extended to the social status quo, represented by the combined rights of worship, assembly, petition, due process, trial by one's peers, and so on. So constitutional conservatism sustains something like the civil society of the eighteenth century even in the face of industrial revolution, mass immigration, urbanization, cold war — changes not only in the scope but also in the very character of our common life.

II

Conservatism must be the crucial feature of any written constitution: Why write it down except to give the machinery it designs and the principles it proclaims stability over the long haul? And yet the Constitution is also a radical document, opening the way for, if not actually stimulating, social change. I want to turn now to the subversive logic of rights, which is, I suppose, the currently fashionable topic, though it is not fashion alone that dictates the turn. In the last several decades, in politics and jurisprudence alike, the Constitution's second text has come fully into its own. Instead of a set of restraints on the operation of the state machine, the Bill of Rights is more and more taken to describe the purpose of the machine. Once it was said that the government must not violate individual rights as it goes about its business. Now it is said that the chief business of government is to realize individual rights. Rights these days are less things that people actually have than things that they have a right to have — and therefore ought to have *right now*.[6] What lies behind this sea-change is the discovery (and the self-discovery) of the invisible men and women of twentieth-century civil society. For these people, the first text of the Constitution provides an agency, and the second text a mandate, for social change.

So the Constitution facilitates the defense but also the transformation of civil society. I want to look now at four different sorts of social and political action through which the transformation is attempted. Though the list is logically neat, I don't claim that it is exhaustive. It begins with civil society, then moves on to the state, on the assumption that the transformative work is commonly initiated by individuals and groups who then seek the help of one or another part of the governmental machine.

First, collective action to alter the existing patterns of ownership, hierarchy, command and obedience: the work of parties and mass movements. Here the Bill of Rights functions primarily to enable groups of citizens to assemble, organize, petition, and so on. But it is also said, as in the civil rights movement for example, that oppressed and excluded men and women don't in fact enjoy the rights enumerated in the Bill and will never enjoy them until the social order has been transformed. So the Bill provides a reason as well as an enabling framework for transformation. The most significant fact about political action of this sort, however, is its relative lack of success. Despite many beginnings, moments of high hope, and real achievements along the way, the social order and all its hierarchies are more or less intact. One reason for this (relative) failure is the very diversity of civil society and the protection accorded to diversity by the Bill of Rights. This group, let's say, supports a certain reform; another group opposes it; and both act with equal right (to assemble, organize, petition, and so on) even if one side is "right" in terms of rights theory. Another perhaps more important reason is that diversity does not express itself only in differences of opinion but also in differences in power. Enabling is equal, but in most cases of political or social conflict the two sides are not equally able. Effective political organization requires resources as well as constitutional entitlements — and those who already have resources are likely to be constitutionally entitled to them. So the conservatism of rights subverts their inherent subversiveness.

Second, individual action to alter one's own relationships without waiting for a more general social transformation. If collective action takes the form that Albert Hirschman calls "voice," individual action commonly takes the form of "exit."[7] It is marked by a radically individualist and separatist spirit: emigration, secession, divorce, resignation, disengagement. The spirit, again, has religious origins—in the idea of a conscience that can never be locked up, tied down, coerced or bound, except with reference to a personal God. The post-Protestant individual claims a similar freedom, usually without the exception. Privacy is the most cherished individual right, and it is on its behalf that the Supreme Court has shaped a new right "constructively" out of all the explicit rights of the Bill and guaranteed the integrity of a private realm. The construction seems legitimate enough; one can't protect rights of association without acknowledging rights of dissociation. But just as the "unencumbered self" of liberal theory was once thought to bear the encumbrances of God, so he has ever since been thought ready and willing to encumber himself. If he protested against one obligation, he assumed another; left one church, joined another; divorced one spouse, married another. It would be a very great change indeed in the pattern of social relationships if the "unencumbered self" of theory were to emerge in practice as the radically unattached individual—standing alone but with the very best legal standing, the ward, as it were, of the Court.

Third, governmental action for the sake of social reform or transformation (seconding and supporting the collective efforts of parties and movements within civil society). This is exactly the sort of action that was supposed to be constrained by the Bill of Rights, the second text setting limits on the powers created by the first, without however making it impossible to exercise those powers. But the government can act on behalf of rights as well as be subject to their constraint. The classic example in recent times is the enforcement of school desegregation in the name of "equal protection." Wherever rights are systematically violated, government must seek a systematic remedy, and it is unlikely that the remedy can consist entirely of prohibitions and preventions. Positive action will commonly be required, institutional rearrangements, new governmental policies and social practices. Given the regime of checks and balances, this sort of thing is achieved, if it is achieved at all, very slowly. Competing interests inside the state machine, like competing interests in civil society, inhibit social transformation.

Fourth, governmental action for the sake of individual freedom (seconding and supporting private efforts). What is involved here is precisely prohibition and prevention, the annulment of repressive legislation, the hindrance of hindrances to free choice and private willfulness. Here the Court has been the most important agency, authorized by the second text to oppose all other agencies of government. Its achievements are impressive: It has banned prayer in the public schools, legalized abortion, virtually abolished the censorship of art and literature, extended the right of conscientious objection to nonreligious persons, established the private realm. Other agencies are also active, as in recent legislation (at the state rather than the federal level) reforming the procedures for divorce and divorce settlements, so as to make divorce much easier than it once was and also, apparently, to shift resources from families and children to single individuals, mostly men.[8] One can be happy or unhappy about these achievements or happy about some and unhappy about others, but they do derive in a fairly consistent way from the second text: They are generated by taking rights and the rights-bearing individual seriously. As soon as one does that, the rights that we actually exercise fade in significance before the rights that we might exercise, if only the powerful machine provided by the first text can be harnessed for the job.

What this brief survey suggests is the strongly individualist bias that the second text introduces into the Constitution as a whole. Of course, it is generally true in every human society that individuals are more capable of changing their own situation than of changing the social order, but I don't think that there are many societies in which the possibilities for individual change are so large and so radical that they function as a virtual substitute for social change. Nor can there be many societies in which the government, as incapable in the United States as anywhere else of structural reform, can so easily be enlisted in defense of individual freedom, that is to say, in defense of protest, separation, and privacy. Of the four sorts of action that I have described, the second and fourth, where single individuals are the active agents or immediate beneficiaries, are culturally preferred and constitutionally favored — most likely, therefore, to be effective. It is easy enough to think of individuals and whole classes of individuals for whom they are not (yet) effective, whose rights are not (yet) taken seriously. But the social and constitutional tendency is clear.

We might describe that tendency, programmatically, in the language of "critical legal theory." It represents, as Roberto Unger writes of his own program, a "super-liberalism" which "pushes the liberal premises about state and society, about freedom from dependence and governance of social relations by the will, to the point at which they merge into a large ambition: the building of a social world less alien to a self that can always violate the generative rules of its own mental or social constructs."[9] This is the old Protestant scheme restated (in state-of-the-art theoretical language), with the same self at the center, who can always scruple at doing what, only a short time ago, he solemnly promised to do. It seems that the self is known now by his will rather than his conscience, but he poses familiar problems nonetheless. Doesn't the dissidence of his dissent, the constant violation of generative rules, get in the way of the larger enterprise, "building a social world"? Unger hedges his bets when he hopes for nothing more than a world "less alien" to the eternally transgressive self. Indeed, it is hard to imagine any sort of *social* world in which this self won't be constrained to some degree, in which, therefore, he won't continue to feel himself alien, something less than Rousseau's citizen bound only by his own will. What is the program, then, for this "something less"? What account can we give of the legitimate constraints on dissidence and violation?

III

We might respond to these questions simply by pointing to the first text of the Constitution. There the government is authorized to tax its citizens, to punish them for violating its laws, to regulate their commercial relations, to raise armies and make war. But this just describes the capabilities of the machine; it doesn't tell us how it is to be operated or for what ends. The ends described in the preamble are too inclusive to be very helpful: "establish Justice, insure domestic Tranquility, provide for the common defense, promote the general Welfare, and secure the blessings of Liberty for ourselves and our Posterity." On a certain reading of the liberal tradition, the last two of these stand in sharp contradiction to one another: The more liberty is secured for individuals, the less general will welfare be. I don't want to insist that this is the only correct reading of the tradition, but certainly the actual experience of protestantism, separatism, and privatization makes it hard to say what an adjective like "general," or even a plural pronoun like "our," might mean. Is there anything that is so importantly general, so deeply ours, that we might for its sake discourage protest, separation, and privacy?

A hard question. I assume that most Americans are not prepared—certainly, I am not—to give up any of the rights enumerated in the second text. But one of the chief reasons for valuing those rights, it seems to me, is that they facilitate the first and third forms, the collective and cooperative forms, of social action. They enable groups of citizens who share some religious or political or economic understanding or interest to organize themselves, to act on their understanding and defend their interest. The assumption of the Constitution, of the two texts taken together, is that people will have different ideas, first of all about eternal life and salvation and then about the preamble's list: justice, tranquility, defense, welfare, and liberty. The theoretical justification for these differences is individualist in character; hence the bias of the text. But the expected activity was collective: When one asserts "the right of the people peacefully to assemble," one expects assemblies — not litigious individuals tracked by lawyers, but gatherings, meetings, caucuses, and party conventions; not legal argument, but political debate; not briefs, but pamphlets.

The privatizing effects of the Bill of Rights were almost certainly not anticipated by the authors of the Bill. What they had in mind, as I have already suggested, was the existing diversity of American society. This was indeed a separatist society, composed, that is, of people who had literally separated themselves from old world states and churches. Once again, these people justified their separation on grounds of private conscience, the moral knowledge each one of them shared with his God. In practice, however, they shared this knowledge among themselves too. And so the diversity to which they gave rise was a diversity of groups. The groups rested on individual consent, but they *rested* on consent with some confidence and security. That's why it was so easy to assign conscientious objector status on the basis of membership.[10] The separatism of American life did not mean, or was not taken to mean, that Americans were frivolous in their associations. On the contrary, they made weighty decisions and formed stable groups; hence the actions of these groups, their assemblies and petitions and, by extension, their rallies, demonstrations, marches, and strikes, were worthy of constitutional protection. Individuals with consciences and interests formed groups with purposes. And since the purpose of many of these groups was and is to convince the rest of us to live in a certain way, to think of justice, tranquility, and so on, in these terms rather than those, the socializing effects of conscience and interest are extensive and far reaching.

Yet this is true only so long as it seems both necessary and possible to convince the rest of us to live in a certain way. There is always this alternative: to live that way oneself "without tarrying for the magistrate," as seventeenth-century Protestants argued — or for anyone else. Despite its anticipation of collective action, the Constitution has turned out to favor something else, nicely summed up in the twentieth-century maxim about "doing your own thing." Imagine now a civil society founded on this maxim, a literal diversity of indi-

viduals, this one and that one and that one and that one, not an assembly or a congregation or a community but something more like
what Sartre calls a "series."[11] Of course, doing your own thing does
not mean living in isolation, for some of the things one wants to do
can't be done alone. People will still come together for conversation,
love, worship, and even the defense of common interests. But these
unions are likely to be temporary and unstable, given the radical individualism on which they are based. The example of religious cult-
ism in the United States today suggests that they are also likely to be
frivolous. Cults are as entitled to constitutional protection as
churches and congregations; we would not want a governmental office set up to distinguish between serious and silly religiosity. But
that is not a reason to rejoice in the advance of silliness. Similarly,
the growing number of people living alone—living in "single person
households," in the census phrase—are entitled to exactly the same
protection that families get against, say, "unreasonable searches and
seizures," but that is no reason to rejoice in the advance of solitude
and dissociation.

A Sartrean "series," a dissociated society, is a limiting case.
Sartre's example is a queue, and the example makes it obvious that a
whole society organized on the serial principle is not possible: Without some background solidarity, every queue would turn into a me-
lee. Similarly, a society composed entirely of single-family households and religious cults would have no cohesion at all, would not,
in fact, be a "society." I am describing tendencies, not established
realities. Still, it is worth asking what resistance we can put up to
these tendencies.

It is not the divisiveness of dissociation that is worrying. Rousseau
argued long ago that if a society had to be divided, then multiplying
the divisions would reduce their force and salience: A host of secondary associations is second best to none at all.[12] In my limiting case,
however, the host equals the total number of citizens; every individual member of society is self-associated, primary in his own eyes, secondary in everyone else's. The conflicts among individuals are then
too dispersed and trivial to threaten the stability of social life, but
they are also too dispersed and trivial to energize social life. A society
in which political parties and interest groups quarrel about the common defense and the general welfare is, however bitter the quarrels,
a society whose members are forced to think about what is common
and what is general. They are mobilized for democratic politics, that
is, for public work of many different kinds, more or less useful, more

dissociated society all work is apolitical, private, and (mostly) uninteresting.

Is there some way to bring rights-bearing individuals together, to enhance the possibilities for collective action? Here the Supreme Court is not likely to be much help; the second text that it enforces doesn't press in this direction, whatever the anticipation of its authors. Consulting a lawyer and writing a brief will not right now (though it sometimes might) advance the cause of association. Perhaps the Constitution as a whole, conceived as the sacred text of a civil religion, might help. Indeed, the Constitution is the sacred text of our civil religion, but the seminary in which the text is studied, expounded, and interpreted is the law school; the chief ritual observance is litigation; and litigation serves most importantly to enhance the second and fourth forms, the privatizing forms, of social action. We can, of course, celebrate the diversity that the Constitution fosters and protects. It is harder to celebrate radical dissociation. Can we be knit together by our mutual acceptance of separation? A society that respects individualism can also respect itself and value the legal structure through which it operates. I am less sure about a society whose members are merely tolerant of (or resigned to) each other's isolation. Are they grateful to be allowed, when they please, to part company and be left alone, or do they yearn (secretly) for an unconstitutional solidarity?

Yearnings like that can be dangerous, and yet I want to argue that a decent society requires not only individual rights but also group solidarities and the pluralist and democratic politics that groups make possible. Democracy itself is a value sufficiently general and sufficiently ours to warrant state action against the long-term effects of privatization. If the Court defends and extends the regime of rights, then perhaps it is the task of Congress to look for ways of strengthening the internal life, the jurisdictional reach, and the cohesiveness of secondary associations. I have no list of measures in mind; I would only recall the way in which the Wagner Act facilitated the organization of labor unions in the 1930s or the way in which matching grants to private welfare agencies have made it possible today for religious groups to run an extensive system of daycare centers, hospitals, and nursing homes. The Constitution is biased toward individual rights, and perhaps it should be; but constitutional power exists to balance the bias or to counter some of its effects. And just as the Court's commitment to rights generates new rights and pushes separatism beyond the actually existing separateness of civil society, so Congress's commitment to group solidarity ought to generate new groupings and new experiences of collective action: worker-owned factories, health cooperatives, experimental schools, neighborhood alliances, and so on.

It should not be the goal of congressional action, however, to create a single, all-encompassing solidarity. That was what the Bill of Rights, and especially the First Amendment with its no-establishment clause, was designed to prevent—for the sake of a civil society that is probably still lively and diverse enough to resist the creation. The Bill was designed, indeed, to protect the existing states as well as the existing churches, interest groups, and families, and perhaps we need to look again to our federalist past if we are to revitalize associational life. The states do not seem at this moment the best possible units for collective action, but no one can predict at what level of politics or society the best units might be found. We have to ask: Where is there some effective demand for organizational structure and common effort? Where might there be an enthusiastic response to governmental initiative? Where are the creative forces in our society that might benefit, as the labor movement once benefited, from political authorization? Insofar as these questions have answers, we have a political agenda and a constitutional structure within which to pursue it. If it ever happens that they have no answers, we are probably beyond constitutional help.

I argued at the beginning of this paper that the original Constitution designed a state and the Bill of Rights reflected a society. The purpose of the Bill was to make the constituent elements of that society inaccessible to the state. Its authors thought those elements, rights-bearing individuals, above all, to be strong and creative. Today those same individuals, carrying those same rights (or new rights of the same sort), look very different: Dissociation renders them weak and passive. So it makes sense to call the state to the rescue of civil society and then to search for effective means of rescue—for the state is the only constitutionally specified agent of collective action and the only agent that might, conceivably, be pregnant with additional agents. I need only say, finally, that when the state acts in this way it can only act subject to its internal checks and balances, which now include all the rights that the Court enforces. But I don't think it is merely a political trick (though it may be tricky) to look for ways of limiting protestantism, separatism, and privatization without violating individual rights.

NOTES

1. See the *Anti-Federalists*, ed. Cecelia M. Kenyon (Indianapolis: Bobbs-Merrill, 1966), pp. xxxviii, lxx, 186–89, 193–233.

2. Alexander Hamilton, *Federalist* 78.

3. The standard example of this argument is C. B. Macpherson, *The Political Theory of Possessive Individualism: Hobbes to Locke* (Oxford: The Clarendon Press, 1962).

4. Michael J. Sandel, *Liberalism and the Limits of Justice* (Cambridge: Cambridge University Press, 1982).

5. A. S. P. Woodhouse, ed., *Puritanism and Liberty* (London: J. M. Dent and Sons, 1938), pt. 1 ("The Putney Debates"), p. 34.

6. See the arguments of Ronald Dworkin, *Taking Rights Seriously* (Cambridge, Mass.: Harvard University Press, 1977).

7. Albert Hirschman, *Exit, Voice, and Loyalty: Responses to Decline in Firms, Organizations, and States* (Cambridge, Mass.: Harvard University Press, 1970).

8. See Lenore Weitzman, *The Divorce Revolution* (New York: Free Press, 1986).

9. Roberto Unger, *The Critical Legal Studies Movement* (Cambridge, Mass.: Harvard University Press, 1986), p. 41.

10. Michael Walzer, *Obligations: Essays on Disobedience, War, and Citizenship* (Cambridge, Mass.: Harvard University Press, 1970), chap. 6.

11. Jean-Paul Sartre, *Critique of Dialectical Reason, I, Theory of Practical Ensembles*, trans. Allan Sheridan-Smith (London: N.L.B., 1976), pp. 256ff.

12. Jean-Jacques Rousseau, *The Social Contract*, trans G. D. H. Cole (New York: E. P. Dutton, 1950), bk. 2, chap. 3.

7

POLITICAL "REALISM" AND THE PROGRESSIVE DEGRADATION OF CITIZENSHIP: A QUIET CONSTITUTIONAL CRISIS

ROBERT E. CALVERT

> The great Statesman, like the great moral leader, is one who appeals to the higher emotions, to principle, to self-restraint, not to selfishness and appetite.
> —*A. Lawrence Lowell*

> I'll tell you what wins votes. Whatever puts money in here [his wallet] wins votes, and whatever takes money out of here loses votes.
> —*George Bush*

> A political actor, be he good or evil, does not deal in unreality. Rather, he creates realities that matter. . . . An actor not only projects, he causes his audience to project certain qualities.
> —*George Will*

> If men define situations as real, they are real in their consequences.
> —*W. I. Thomas*

It sometimes happens in the public life of a nation that a casual, offhand remark by a political figure reveals with stark clarity one of the master assumptions not only of his or her entourage, party, or class, but, more or less, of the age. Such a moment occurred during the 1984 presidential campaign. Speaking to "about 2,000 cheering Re-

For helpful criticisms and comment on this essay in its various drafts, I am grateful to James Cooper, Byron Daynes, Jean Elshtain, Maria Falco, Ralph Gray, David Greenstone, Michael Novak, Ralph Raymond, and Bruce Stinebrickner. Especially valuable were the hard and good questions raised by my student assistants, Douglas Driemeier, Donald Featherstone, and Vikash Yadav, whose critical presence I am happy to acknowledge as nothing short of collegial.

publicans" in Ohio in the midst of the campaign, Vice-President George Bush suggested that Ohioans felt themselves to be part of a national economic recovery brought about by the Reagan administration. Then, in what must have been a theatrical moment, Mr. Bush removed his wallet from his pocket and declared, quoting James Rhodes, a former governor of Ohio, that the only issue in a campaign is the "pocketbook"—"who is putting money in and who is taking it out." "One reason Ronald Reagan is going to get re-elected," he predicted, "is because he's putting something in and the other people are taking something out."[1]

This striking display of tough-minded political realism did not escape the notice of Geraldine Ferraro, Mr. Bush's opponent. Ms. Ferraro was quick to attack Bush's way of making his point—brandishing his wallet—as well as the point itself, charging that "that single gesture of selfishness tells us more about the true character of this administration than all their apple pie."[2]

For all anyone cared—the incident was not widely reported and provoked no editorial comment—Bush could have ignored Ferraro's charge. This was hardly the first time the Reagan administration had been attacked for encouraging, often by its own example, the purely self-regarding instincts of the American people. The great wave of indifference with which the vice-president's remark was met suggested that the nation had lost its capacity to be shocked. Yet "selfishness" is a strong word, and the vice-president evidently thought it could not go unanswered. Ignoring the thrust of Ferraro's charge, Bush countered that

> the opposition goes around buying off every single special interest group in sight with promises our nation can't afford. And then they get all . . . preachy about selfishness. If they're talking about greed, they ought to talk about the greed of big government, which under the last administration knew absolutely no bounds.

Continuing as though Ferraro had maligned the American voter, he defended not the Reagan administration, the object of Ferraro's attack, but the American people:

> The opposition talks as if it were immoral to want to take care of your own family, loved ones, and work toward the good life and maybe buy a new car or get a mortgage on a house or save up for your children's education. We've got news for them—

that is the American dream. There's nothing wrong about it [at] all; freedom, opportunity, family, faith, fair play—that's what America is all about. And if they don't understand it, it's too darn bad.[3]

Returning to the issue at the end of the campaign, Ferraro directly disputed Bush's emphasis on voter self-interest:

George Bush has said this election is only about putting money in the voters' wallets. Of course we care about money, but that's only one thing, not everything, Americans care about. We care about peace, equal opportunity, and the one thing our opponents just don't understand is that we care about each other.[4]

I

What are we to make of the Bush-Rhodes view of the American voter and of the correlative conception of the American Dream? We might begin by noting again that despite the gravity of such issues, especially as the nation moved toward the Bicentennial of its Constitution, this exchange between Bush and Ferraro received virtually no attention at the time, either from the news media, other political figures, or interested onlookers. Possibly it seemed to be commonplace campaign rhetoric, merely a reiteration of hackneyed themes by both sides and hence "not news."

The themes of that campaign aside, it is surely not news that voters will reward the party in power if times are good and punish it if times are hard, or that Americans in general do have the aspirations Bush sums up as the American Dream. Democrats as well as Republicans, liberals as well as conservatives know these basic facts of American political life. Nor is it remarkable that the typical American can be held to have a practical, or "utilitarian," bent when it comes to life in general and to government in particular. These familiar facts would seem to make of the vice-president's pronouncements something like truisms—again, not worth reporting.

Reporters might at least have noticed, however, that such "realism" about what moves voters has rarely been articulated so openly by a politician of Mr. Bush's elevated status, certainly not in recent times. For a parallel, one would have to return to 1920s Normalcy or to the cynicism and crassness of the Gilded Age, only to find that even in those nadirs of the American public spirit the politicians of the day tried to keep up at least the appearance of high-mindedness. What seems new, even shocking, about the vice-president's assertion, when seen against the backdrop of American history and political culture, is that it is so candid, indeed brazen; so stripped of euphemism; so indifferent, say, to the question of social justice or to ideology or party loyalty; so totally devoid of any gesture toward civic responsibility; so exclusively centered on what has been only a part of the traditional meaning assigned to membership in the American polity and of the rights, obligations, and expectations associated with that membership. In a couple of sentences and one theatrical gesture, the vice-president had reduced American citizenship, a complex political and moral status with a rich history, to a single, material, individualistic, and self-regarding dimension.

It will not do to try to soften the impact of the statement about wallets by invoking the family and the American Dream. Mr. Bush's victory in that unremarked little debate seems only to provide substance for some of Tocqueville's worst fears about American egalitarian individualism, apprehensions inspired precisely because this new phenomenon, the individualist, retreated to his "little society" of "family and friends" and left society at large to fend for itself.[5] Look to see in the vice-president's understanding of the American Dream, with its foundation exclusively in economic self-interest, whether there is any room for the American democratic penchant for political freedom, or for the cultivation of those institutions and beliefs that for Tocqueville served as a barrier to majority tyranny and administrative despotism, or for the doctrine of "self-interest properly understood." Where in this picture of the family-as-consumption-unit can one discern the political tie that once was thought to bind Americans into a republic? In this truncated version of our public philosophy there is only one positive reference to anything having to do with government and politics — a fleeting mention of a providing (if not providential) president a grateful people will surely return to power, a paternal presence looming benignly and remotely over a prospering nation. Surely Tocqueville would not have been reassured by the spectacle of such a people governed by such a figure as he pondered the health and prospects of American democracy.

Having said all this, I want immediately to caution critics of George Bush and his administration against deriving comfort from the analysis I present here; if what I say has any merit, we confront in this particular expression a point of view very much in the mainstream of contemporary American political culture. I hope in what follows to show why it is indeed so commonplace in our time to see voters not as citizens but as "individuals" concerned only with their own economic well-being and, similarly, why it is so easy to describe the American Dream as utterly lacking political content. There should be no comfort in this for any of us.[6]

It is already evident that this now-conventional voter, and the correlative vision of the American Dream, could be cited by the other essayists in this volume as disturbing confirmation that their concerns for the well-being of American constitutional democracy are not imaginary. Such a voter may be seen to represent the triumph of Jefferson's hedonistic or humanist liberalism, as David Greenstone sees it, over the reformed or public-spirited liberalism of John Adams. Such a voter represents in principle the final privatization and emancipation of Michael Walzer's "protestant" individual from any and all restraints, including the inevitable restraints of democratic politics—to the point that both of Walzer's texts of the Constitution would seem to be irrelevant. We have an awful caricature of Jean Elshtain's "exquisitely social" individual, then, the sort of "citizen" who, devoted only to personal and family welfare, will find incomprehensible the notion of a common good urged by Robert Bellah. Indeed, given the self-absorbed preoccupation with consumption, it is hard to imagine a voter so oriented as the individual filled with the spirit of enterprise important to Michael Novak.

We are partially reassured on hearing, from Michael Walzer, that these images of a thoroughly privatized citizen and an impoverished politics are only tendencies and not accomplished facts, an observation that applies, fortunately, with even greater force to the vice-president's conception of what wins elections. I say this because it is important to note that Bush's statement about why voters vote as they do is, in our time anyway, false—not an overgeneralization, not an exaggeration of the truth, not an overstatement of a basically sound analysis, but, in its unqualified form, simply and radically false.[7]

If the point were only that most Americans, most of the time, tend to decide whom to vote for on the basis of how they are faring economically—or even that they generally allow their economic position to eclipse other and competing interests and concerns they may have as citizens as they cast their votes—one could cite much evidence in support of that position. But that is not the position of those who speak in this vein.

The vice-president, for example, is not generalizing about voter behavior as a political scientist might—indeed, is not making an "empirical statement" or presenting a "refutable hypothesis" at all.

Rather, it would seem, instead of bad political science, the assertion about the pocketbook voter is something quite different. On the one hand, candidate Bush, on the stump, is articulating what must be seen as some rather conventional American folk wisdom about how people behave in politics, saying "what everybody knows," with the confident assurance that what he says will be well received. He is communicating with his audience on the basis of what in Parsonian sociology is called a shared "belief system." On the other hand, his unqualified assertion about what moves the voter can *also* be seen as a kind of philosophical or theoretical claim, a declaration indeed about "human nature" in politics; his voter is reminiscent of the "natural man" imagined by the great social-contract thinkers of the seventeenth and eighteenth centuries, who in one way or other made a point of telling us, as Rousseau said, to "lay facts aside" in understanding what they were about.[8] In neither case, whether folk wisdom or crude political philosophy, is Bush's statement such as to be considered more or less true when measured against the facts, against what actual people actually do. It would not have occurred to the vice-president to offer evidence for his claim about the significance of the pocketbook in elections or for anyone in his audience to ask for it.[9]

Whatever the ontological status of the kind of voter revealed in Bush's remark, he seems more than vaguely familiar. We think we have met him before, or at any rate some version of him, his ancestor, so to speak, in other times in American history and not only as Tocqueville's individualist or as a shade of the Grant or Harding eras. Indeed, so American does he seem that he may be thought to have come over on the Mayflower. Surely John Winthrop was speaking to that kind of person, or to that person in each of his listeners, as he laid out his "Modell of Christian Charity" on board the Arbella — warning of the fate that would befall them if they "fell to embrace this world" and lost sight of the main (but not the only) reason they had come to New England. Winthrop again might be thought to have confronted the ancestor of the late twentieth-century voter when he reminded his constituents, in his famous "Speech to the General Court," that "natural" liberty, the liberty to do just as you please without regard for what is right or for the well-being of others, is a false and pernicious kind of liberty and quite incompatible with the natural and moral necessity of living together in communities.

The American revolutionaries were no less aware of a forerunner of this creature as they asserted, anxiously if bravely, that as individual citizens and as a people they were capable of the self-discipline, public spiritedness, devotion to the public good—in a word, the re-publican virtue—required of them if they were to govern themselves without a king. Building on their Puritan heritage and blending it with the republicanism of Machiavelli and Montesquieu and the Whiggism of eighteenth-century England, their elaborate paeans of praise to republican virtue bespoke as well their fear of their own proclivities for selfish, antirepublican, and unpatriotic kinds of vice.

Perhaps, we think, we can most clearly see the kind of citizen the vice-president seemed to have in mind in Madison's doleful specula-tions on "human nature," as he and the other Framers struggled to fashion a constitution suitable for a people fallen, as it were, from republican grace—a people, they believed, whose civic virtue had at best been much exaggerated. When Madison contemplated ordi-nary Americans—the majority of his countrymen—he was less im-pressed by their willingness to sacrifice their personal interests for the common good than by their willingness to "vex and oppress each other" in their own interest.[10] Left to their own devices, which in-cluded, Madison believed, a conception of republicanism imper-fectly grounded in human nature and a correspondingly chaotic politics, the noble ideals of the Revolution seemed fated for disaster.

Yet for all the apparent familiarity, we really do not find the soli-tary, purely self-interested individual in Puritanism, in revolution-ary republicanism, or in Madisonian constitutional theory. At best we find him in these earlier American conceptions of the human person only as an intimation, a constant and fearful possibility, the dark side of the soul, embedded in and hence merely a dimension of a whole human being—a threat to the very life of the "errand into the wilderness," the Revolution, the Republic and also a challenge to religion, to revolutionary zeal and practice, to republican educa-tion, and to statecraft. Indeed, when we consider that Winthrop, the Revolutionaries, and Madison were preaching (literally in Win-throp's case) *against* such a man, seeking not just to "domesticate" him, as the vice-president does in his response to Geraldine Ferraro, but to civilize him, to see his essence as a human being not in his merely natural but in his civic self, we may want to conclude that Bush's voter is not present *at all* in early American political culture.

Viewed the other way around, if from some merely Natural Man you took away Winthrop's preoccupation with a close-knit commu-nity, the revolutionaries' Spirit of '76, or the remaining virtue that Madison allowed to the American common man, what you got was surely not Bush's voter. In the case of each of these earlier American concerns about character, what remained when the defining characteristics of the citizen were wholly absent was something wild and uncontrollable, vicious in the extreme, worse (for Winthrop) than an animal; what you got was the turbulent mob of Federalist nightmares — not the rather tame (if corrupt) and predictable egoist portrayed by the vice-president. More than this, we have to see the vice-president's pronouncement, given its appearance in a political campaign aimed at renewing the legitimacy of the American political order, as a kind of reverse jeremiad — an endorsement (if not a celebration) of the least noble part of the American character, a contribution, indeed, to the very corruption of the American electorate he cites as promising his reelection.

II

George Bush's voter did not spring full blown from the head of George Bush. Governor James Rhodes, the immediate source, did not arrive at such a politically denatured conception of the American citizen on his own or spontaneously. That the "2,000 Republicans" cheered and the journalists yawned suggests something more fundamental. To repeat, in his remarks about the American voter and Dream George Bush voiced an assumption of the *age*, and not a point of view peculiar to himself or his party. In this essay I am not interested in George Bush's politics but in *our* politics; Bush's remarks are important not because they were uttered by George Herbert Walker Bush but because his view of what is ultimately "real" in our politics is so widely shared.[11] That he was also the vice-president and hence unavoidably speaking with the authority of his office is perhaps significant if we think about the effect of his remarks on his listeners. The point here, however, is only that Mr. Bush is plausibly an American representative of his time.

He at any rate seems to express our sense of reality. In a famous chapter of *Democracy in America*, Tocqueville observes that the Americans of Jacksonian America had unconsciously adopted the "philosophical approach" of Descartes, unconsciously, that is, because they had never read Descartes. Spurning books and systems, deferring to no aristocracy, Americans doubted everything but the "witness of their own eyes" and relied only on their "individual effort and judgment" as the source of certain knowledge.[12] If Tocqueville were to examine Americans of today, and in particular George Bush's remark about the only thing that counts in an election, he might well conclude that his favorite democrats had exchanged Descartes for Jeremy Bentham as their philosophical guide. When we want to talk about what human beings are really like, we intuitively abstract them, as Bentham did, from any and all social contexts; and when we want to report our conclusions about human nature, we unswervingly declare "man" to be nothing more nor less than Bentham's utility maximizer. No broad experience of actual human beings is necessary to produce this conviction. Anyone doubting this need only engage beginning college students in an open-ended discussion of "human nature." Innocent of history (as was Bentham), to say nothing of anthropology, they "know" that "man" naturally seeks to maximize his pleasures and minimize his pains and generally to "better his condition," and they know this *before* they take the introductory course in economics or behavioral psychology.

Bush's voter, let us be clear, is just such a Benthamite abstraction. As presented he is a pure type, not a part, dimension, or aspect of a larger, more complex human person; he is purely, simply, radically devoid of the usual range of characteristics that suggest the whole person — a "realistic" fiction with most of the reality left out. In particular, he is wholly unaffected by that wide range of cultural learnings political scientists sometimes call political socialization. Indeed, those complex and subtle understandings, often all jumbled together, that somehow tell us what it means to be a good person, a good American, and a good citizen, form no part of his conception of himself. This suggests that if we are to understand this socially unconstituted voter we have to see him, strictly speaking, as "non-American," as existing essentially outside of American history but also, in a sense, as "un-American"— surely in conflict with the traditions and culture that inform and sustain our political life.

For all that, he is familiar. We recognize him not because we've met him in earlier incarnations in American political culture, though individuals approximating the model have surely existed, nor because he is so plausibly "seen" in today's politics, nor because we think our experience confirms his presence as we observe Ed Meese, Michael Deaver, Pentagon weapons procurers, Ivan Boesky, HUD bureaucrats, S&L criminals, or some yuppie we particularly dislike. He is so familiar to us, so unnewsworthy, because he is the centerpiece of a well-known *theory* of human nature in the modern Western world we Americans seem especially to prize. Not just a figment of George Bush's imagination and no mere creature of media cynicism, he is none other than the archetypal Enlightenment Individual, and a thoroughly modernized one at that. He is the Eco-

nomic Man of Econ. 1A, who more recently has taken on new life as
the self-interested voter in so-called public or rational-choice theory.
The vice-president's tough-minded, unsentimental, bottom-line
"realism," then, is a reification of an ahistorical, merely hypothetical, intuitively perceived, theoretical construct.

We next have to ask how it is that in a presidential campaign
speech, appealing to such an unreal theorist's fantasy, to such a textbook abstraction, has come to be regarded as not merely the last
word in realism but as something of a cliché. How has it happened
that one of the most extravagant and radical flights of the theoretical imagination in Western political theory has come to be regarded
as obvious (if disquieting) common sense — an operative bit of American political folklore?

III

A revived interest in the 1980s in free-market ideology is no doubt
the immediate source of this unreal realism. Virtually silenced by
nearly two generations of a dominant welfare-state liberalism,
American liberalism's "conservative" variant could once again wax
theoretical under Ronald Reagan — and could again seek to create a
real world to correspond to its putatively eternal, if hypothetical and
abstract, verities. When the "bottom line" has become a metaphor
for what Marxists used to call the "last analysis," it is perhaps not
surprising that the irreducible truth about politics should be expressed with the double-lined certitude of the accountant.

The laissez-faire renaissance notwithstanding, there is nothing
specifically or distinctively conservative (or even Republican) about
Bush's voter.[13] On the contrary, the politics appropriate to such a
figure — a "politics" focused exclusively on what's-in-it-for-me-and-
my-family — derives, ultimately, I want to argue, from the tradition
of American reform, from sources in our history and culture usually
thought to be on the left. If this unlovely conception of the citizen
seems to flow so obviously from an antigovernment, public-be-
damned, contemporary conservatism, it may be only that one of the
functions of liberals on the American right is to preserve some of the
more unattractive innovations of liberals on the American left.
America is "conservative," Gunnar Myrdal once noted, but "the
principles conserved are liberal, and some, indeed, are radical."[14]

Far from being a product of American conservatism, the corruption represented by Bush's voter is exactly what Herbert Hoover used

to denounce Franklin Roosevelt and the New Deal for trying to produce in the American people. What else was the welfare state, for Hoover, but the wholesale buying of votes, to the destruction of the freedom, independence, and moral fiber of the American people? We may begin by seeing that George Bush, insofar as he represents contemporary "conservatism," has been schooled by FDR, and in reducing the public-spirited citizen to the purely self-regarding voter, Bush is merely expressing a latter-day version of New Deal realism.

At least up to a point. In speaking of the pocketbook we may say that Mr. Bush went not perhaps to the heart but surely to the real core of the political vision, inaugurated by the New Deal, that has dominated American politics since 1932. It is in no way to detract from the idealism and commitment to social justice that made the New Deal such a force in American politics to point out that it was launched from a very material foundation. Indeed, nearly twenty years before Franklin Roosevelt in his Second Inaugural Address saw "one-third of a nation ill-housed, ill-clad, ill-nourished" and promised to do something about it, Herbert Croly, the intellectual architect (if it had one) of the New Deal, had described the American common man's material expectations in terms that made something like the New Deal, given the Great Depression, a virtual necessity.

All Americans, according to Croly, the God-centered Puritans no less than the immigrants of his own day, came to these shores at least in part to better their material lot in life. "With all their professions of Christianity," Croly wrote of his countrymen, "their national idea remains thoroughly worldly. . . . The promise, which bulks so large in their patriotic outlook, is a promise of comfort and prosperity for an ever increasing majority of good Americans."[15] So important had the quest for material well being become to Americans, he noted, that the expectation of it was regarded as a kind of national birthright and a test of political legitimacy itself:

> The success of this democratic political system was indissolubly associated in the American mind with the persistence of abundant and widely distributed economic prosperity. Our democratic institutions became in a sense the guarantee that prosperity would continue to be abundant and accessible. In case the majority of good Americans were not prosperous, there would be grave reasons for suspecting that our institutions were not doing their duty.[16]

In describing the voter and the American Dream as he does, George Bush can plausibly be seen as in the New Deal tradition.

Consider, too, Bush's view of the presidency. "Our democratic institutions," to which Croly referred, preeminently included that office as a consequence of the Roosevelt Revolution. Reflecting on the New Deal in the 1950s, Clinton Rossiter could announce that the presidency had evolved in such a way as to provide informal acknowledgment of Croly's vision of the link between popular material aspirations and democratic political institutions. Not only did the post-New Deal president continue to be the "voice of the people," as he had been since Andrew Jackson, he was now also the "manager of prosperity."[17] It should thus occasion no surprise that in 1984 a president who put money in the voters' wallets is seen as doing his duty and is duly reelected.

The self-regarding voter and largely material American Dream are thus the recognizable if not wholly legitimate offspring of that convenient marriage of Hamiltonian means (a powerful national government) and Jeffersonian ends (popular material well-being) sanctified by Croly's *Promise of American Life*.

Yet they also stand as eloquent criticisms of the failure of the New Deal to go beyond the admittedly pressing material needs of the American people to the nurturing of the civic self. It is hard to escape the conclusion, for example, that the "interest group liberalism" stemming from the New Deal, to use Theodore Lowi's term,[18] failed to link popular material aspirations with what Croly *also* had said was a constant of American political history and culture. Croly had of course been quick to add that material well-being was only half the promise of American life; the land of economic prosperity was also the land of individual freedom and of a personal dignity that could come only from social equality. "America" stood for a way of life that also meant both individual and social improvement:

> The amelioration promised to aliens and to future Americans was to possess its moral and social aspects. The implication was, and still is, that by virtue of the more comfortable and less trammeled lives which Americans were enabled to lead, they would constitute a better society and would become in general a worthier set of men.[19]

And it was for the sake of transforming this promise into a "constructive national purpose" that Croly set forth a theory that would reconcile the American democrat, hitherto "self-reliant, undisciplined, suspicious of authority, equalitarian, and individualistic," exhibiting a "mixture of optimism, fatalism, and conservatism"[20] and overwhelmingly local in his practical attachments if not his patriotic sentiments, with a "national political organization"—that is, with active, positive government. We may not wish to lament the failure of Croly's own technocratic vision to receive full institutional expression in the remainder of the twentieth century, but the point is that, contrary to Croly's hopes for a "worthier set of men," however defined, the development of the American political system was somehow arrested at a rather primitive and material level. A "better" society? We at any rate became a richer one, and, as Croly's sense of irony might have led him to remark, sufficient unto the day was the prosperity thereof.

Indeed, it is hard to escape the conclusion that the New Deal failed to link popular material aspirations with a "constructive social ideal" pursued by a "national organization" and guided by a "noble national purpose," Croly's or anyone else's. It is even harder to believe that the New Deal bequeathed to George Bush a conception of the civic self in any essential consistent with what citizenship meant to the founding generation. But on that subject Croly himself, theorist of the New Deal, was revealingly silent.

It is true that the zeal, dedication, and passion for social justice expressed by and through FDR's Democratic party was not reducible to a bread-and-butter prosperity or to the homeliness of Bush's American Dream. It may also be true, however, that the actual arrival of national prosperity after World War II served to obscure the extent to which a thinly disguised majoritarian selfishness had become tacitly established as a surrogate public philosophy. What if, say, only one-tenth of the nation continues in one way or other to be wretched and the remainder are pretty well off and reasonably content? A Democratic party slogan of 1968—"If you want to continue to live like a Republican, vote Democratic"—gets us part of the way to Bush's voter. A remark at the Republican National Convention in 1972—"The majority of the American people are unyoung, unblack, and unpoor"—takes us the rest of the way.

IV

Yet the ultimate source of this view of the satisfied citizen and of a diminished American Dream, as George Bush's reference to the "special interests" makes us see, is not the New Deal but Croly's own

Progressive era—the New Deal being practically an *ad hoc* or pragmatic extension of Progressivism. Under the gun because of the Great Depression, the New Deal never got around to addressing any but the most pressing and obvious problems and may well have instilled in the American popular consciousness the notion that politics and government were for serving your own or your group's economic interest and for nothing else. If so, the New Deal was but acting out a script prepared by the previous generation of theorists and reformers.

It was not merely that the economic crisis made an essentially material American Dream seem good enough under the circumstances and civic virtue in the citizen a luxury. More than this, the understanding of *reality* generated by the Progressives made any alternative appear as it has ever since, idealistic, naive, out of touch with the facts of life, even threateningly moralistic. For the New Deal to have done much besides attend to the economic crisis, it would have been required not only to transcend itself but also to repudiate some of the most fundamental assumptions of Progressivism.

V

Science, plus technology, plus industry, was surely much of what "progress" meant to the Progressive era. It would be hard to exaggerate the faith in science and expertise that inspired those legions of zealous reformers. A more promising faith for the new century confronting them, science had in principle replaced religion for growing numbers of Americans, certainly those in enlightened leadership circles, as the basis of their world view. And knowledge (science) was power, as Francis Bacon had insisted, power through technology and industry for producing just that material prosperity Croly cited as the *sine qua non* of American political legitimacy. Moreover, the industrial transformation of America also meant national power, internally as the rapid growth of bureaucracy called forth by the regulatory movement brought about a centralization of both political and administrative power and externally as the United States was well on its way to becoming the most powerful, as well as the richest, nation on earth.

Although such progress had indeed transformed American society and economy almost beyond recognition during the half century after the Civil War, the reformers themselves, Mr. Dooley observed, were not making a revolution but only "beating a carpet," attempting to purge what they thought to be an essentially sound system of adventitious corrupting elements, the works, in their view, of evil and designing men.

What Mr. Dooley could not see, what the reformers themselves (Croly possibly excepted) were unable to see, was that they were contributing willy-nilly to the consolidation of the Hamiltonian national State system. The Framers of the Constitution, we should not forget, sought to create not only a more perfect union but, as the Anti-Federalists quickly saw, a more powerful national government, a system of government of potentially great power indeed.

It was Alexander Hamilton who foresaw an industrial America (as opposed to Jefferson's agrarian ideal) and who saw Americans more as factory workers than as independent citizens. It was Hamilton who sought to wed the interests of well-to-do manufacturers to the new national government, who urged the neutralization of state and local political power, who advocated (successfully) that the national government have direct power over individual citizens, who championed a strong presidency over a factionalized congress, and who argued (again, successfully) for a national government (and especially the judiciary) generally removed as far as possible from popular control. Though it was no doubt hard for American capitalists to see the Progressives and later the New Dealers as their benefactors, both eras of reform, while helping generally to realize Hamilton's vision perhaps most importantly served to rationalize and stabilize a "political economy"[21] that otherwise threatened to self-destruct.

The Progressive reformers nevertheless took their carpet beating seriously because they were altogether uncritical believers (very American ones) in the idea of progress. Where the European theorists of the generic idea of progress looked back on the past as a record of darkness, superstition, and oppression, the American Progressives for the most part saw the exact opposite. As Croly wryly noted, his fellow Progressives were inclined to be "protestants," meaning that they cherished a vision of the American political system functionally similar to Luther's conception of the primitive Church. This suggested that "reform" was really a kind of Reformation, a re-forming of the present corrupt system in light of the purity of the original plan of the Framers—a restoration, indeed a "revival." Those great statesmen had discovered for all time Nature's plan for the perfect form of government, which an inattentive citizenry, alas, had allowed to fall under the control of the Unscrupulous. There was thus nothing fundamentally wrong with the American political system; it had simply been corrupted by bad men—the urban bosses, the unprincipled "plutocrats," dishonest politicians in both parties, and the like. Eliminate these corrupting elements by means of the appropriate reforms, and all would be well—that is, would be as the Founding Fathers intended.

Not only was the American past a good and glorious one, it was also uniquely American; though in accord with the dictates of Nature itself, the American political order was also the peculiar possession of the American people. The reformers never doubted Lincoln's belief that if democracy failed in America, it would "perish from this earth." America was truly the last best hope of mankind.

For all the "worldliness" of the American promise, we cannot begin to understand the Progressives or their legacy unless we see that they defined the past, the way of life they thought they remembered and wanted to restore, almost exclusively in terms that are unmistakably *political*. Specifically, viewing the work of the Framers through lenses tinted by Jacksonianism, Progressive Americans saw the struggle against the bosses and the trusts as a struggle for a revived "democracy." If Lincoln had said the Civil War was "somehow caused" by slavery, he was quite certain that the ultimate issue was whether there would survive the "government of the people, by the people, and for the people" that "our fathers" had "brought forth on this continent." With Lincoln's triad of democratic phrases ringing in their ears—the platforms of all three parties in 1912, Republican, Democratic, and Progressive, quoted Lincoln—the Progressives had a political battle cry that embraced the whole of the American way of life, and its name was democracy.

A way of life so conceived, democracy so dedicated, was in deep trouble as it confronted the realities of the new age dawning. The old way of life, the life of rural and small town America, of a rough social equality, of wide open economic opportunity, of small-scale participatory politics, of the vague and shifting boundaries between politics, morality, economic pursuits, and religion—this democracy, as Tocqueville himself foresaw in his warnings about an "aristocracy of manufacturers,"[22] was quite incompatible with the inevitable concentrations of economic, social, and political power of the new industrial society and bureaucratic state. In short, the Hamiltonian system emerging, both cause and effect of progress, was the virtual negation of the past the Progressive crusaders thought they wanted to restore.

The old way of life itself, as Marx and William Graham Sumner in their different ways pointed out, would change quickly enough, as "capitalism" (Marx) or "the industrial organization" (Sumner) transformed the most basic conditions of life and created a world after its own image. "Democracy," however, the complex range of meanings and associations that had defined and legitimated the old way of life, was a more serious problem. The received or traditional meaning of the national creed had become an embarrassment. The new system wanted obedient workers, consumers, and taxpayers, and, when necessary, soldiers; it would have a hard time coping with the traditional American democrat—"self-reliant, undisciplined, suspicious of authority, equalitarian, and individualistic," as Croly described him, which was a good enough picture of the Jacksonian participating citizen. Plainly, "democracy" too had to be transformed, and this the Progressives would achieve without quite knowing what they had done.

As a force for the modernization of American life, as a largely unwitting instrument of consolidated, centralized, national power in a bureaucratic, technological age,[23] the Progressive movement, Janus-faced between past and future, had to discredit an old way of life before it could create a new one. And since that old American way of life had been described—indeed defined—almost exclusively in political terms, as a *republican* and *democratic* as well as a natural and a moral order, the Progressive movement, before it was finished, had effectively undermined where it had not outright destroyed the specifically political legacy of the American past. In particular, the Progressives in effect depoliticized the concept of the good American as they thought about and worked toward the new society, believing all the while that they were only restoring "government of the people, by the people, and for the people" to its rightful place in the American scheme of things. Here a distinction is in order. Although the crusading reformers thus unintentionally contributed to this transformation of democracy and the citizen, it was mainly the work of ostensibly detached intellectuals—and in particular of the newly professionalized social scientists, who quickly assumed a kind of oracular status in American life.[24]

Were trusts and other new forms of organization and concentrated power a violation of the old egalitarian competitive and moral order? No doubt, but there was another way to look at it: With the new and unsentimental economics able to explain "economies of scale," all but the most fervent trust busters were forced to agree that concentration of economic power, bigness per se, was not only not necessarily bad but was in fact part of the very (Hamiltonian) means by which the (Jeffersonian) material aspirations of the

American common man were to be realized. Yet there was both more and less in the old republicanism of Jefferson (even granting his "hedonism") than "making it"—less because republican strictures against "luxury" precluded a quest for *mere* wealth and power and more because Jefferson's republicanism required that citizens be "participators" in their own government, that they be *public* persons.[25] Unfortunately, a corporate economy and a fragmented polity made *that* part of old republicanism, now "democracy," increasingly problematic.

What to do with "democracy" as a *political* way of life? Could there be an understanding of what it meant to a good American that avoided the political altogether? "A democracy is more than a form of government," John Dewey had said; "it is primarily a mode of associated living, of conjoint communicated experience."[26] Ultimately it would be seen as no form of government at all and not much in the way of "associated living" either, as the Progressives came to encourage a view of the "citizen" as "the individual," with "making it" the chief concern. The concept of "democratic capitalism," developed later in the century as a stratagem in corporate public relations, reinforced the point that democracy and hence Americanism was somehow a function of economics. Yet it was the Progressives themselves who had paved the way for this reductionism—for the easy identification of a classic form of government, a "constitution" requiring a common involvement in a politically defined way of life, with an economic system based on individual, material self-interest.[27]

The Progressive theorists propounded a new idea of politics and ultimately of citizenship, in which neither democracy nor republicanism as Americans had understood them made any sense. They did this, moreover, in the time-honored American way, in the guise of an attack on theory and ideas as such. Pragmatism in general and the newly self-conscious discipline of political science in particular, both contributors to what Bernard Crick called the "cult of realism in the Progressive era," set about quietly to divorce democratic politics from any notion of a common good and citizenship itself from any conception of an integrated life. When the new realists were finished, politics could never again be identified with the good, either of the person or of society, and especially not of that quaint relic, the State. In this campaign, it must be said, the practical (and zealous) reformers themselves were unwitting accomplices.

In the first place, the crusaders in the movement approached the task of political reform deeply alienated from both the politics and the government of their day. Government for the most part they deemed properly to be the province of experts, and the age seemed determined to transform all political questions into administrative ones. As for politics, the reformers' many devices for direct democracy bespoke a conviction that parties, legislatures, and courtrooms were irretrievably corrupt — certainly not fit instruments for genuine popular rule. Inevitably, it would seem, "politics" and "political," virtual synonyms for dishonesty, incompetence, and worse, became dissociated in the minds of reformers with the virtue traditionally attaching to the activity appropriate to the citizen. "Politics" and "political" became objects of distaste and moral revulsion. Hence the reputation of the reformers for self-righteousness and of their public action as a crusade.

When the passion for reform subsided, such a politics of redemption and reformation would collapse of its own unfulfilled hopes and expectations — with more than a little help, however, from its ostensible friends, the scientific realists. Serving as the midwife of disillusionment, the new science of politics attacked directly the core of (crusading) Progressive democratic beliefs about good citizenship. Did the reformers exalt civic-mindedness; careful, detached, objective attention to the "issues"; the sacrifice of time, energy, and personal resources for the public good — and this on an increasing number of complex and arcane matters that vexed even the experts? Voting studies could easily show that this "rationalist image of the common man" (Carl Friedrich's term) was largely a "myth." Were the crusaders appalled at the rank selfishness and dirty dealing of the "special interests," whose machinations were a blight on the land and a standing violation of the common good? The "group interpretation of politics" provided by Arthur F. Bentley argued that such group behavior was merely what the political game was all about, that it was unscientific to judge the motives of the groups, and that in any case the "common good" was another of those "myths" with no basis in the observable behavior of groups. Did the reformers talk reverently of the "sovereign" people, and of the "will" of the people? They did so just as the growing economic, social, and ethnic diversity of American society made the notion of a unified popular will wildly at odds with the facts. Democratic citizenship on that model thus was rendered "unrealistic" and those who continued to believe in it naive.

Nor was this all. As the crusaders' conception of the citizen drew heavily on a century of conviction about democracy and the common man, the scientific critique of Populist and then Progressive political revivalism necessarily went further than its ostensible target. There was in fact no room for the old democratic citizen, or for republican virtue, or for the common good, or for a sovereign people (however conceived), in Bentley's scheme of things. In the old order the good citizen, the good American, and the good man or woman had formed a continuum, a unity, a kind of gestalt; in Bentley's political science, however, concerned as it was to be scientific and to accept as real only the observable and the measurable, there were only "roles" and groups of various kinds and nothing more. A realist, scientific political science was simply uninterested in what would later be dismissed as "normative" concepts, concepts derived from an older political science and from a traditional American public philosophy now derided by Bentley as "soul-stuff." As Charles A. Beard put it, to be scientific meant you had to separate the study of politics from "theology, ethics, and patriotism," which together could be taken as summing up traditional American beliefs.[28] And like Marx (or at any rate Engels), Bentley also relegated the "state" to his own museum of antiquities, perhaps alongside "the individual," who for Bentley was real only as a member of a group. "When the groups are adequately stated, everything is stated," Bentley claimed. "When I say everything I mean everything. The complete description is the complete science."[29]

Between the moralistic crusaders who thought of the citizen in such rarified and demanding terms as virtually to guarantee disillusionment and the amoral political scientists who appeared simply to define the citizen out of existence, there would seem to be little left of the traditional American democrat. Yet it was not enough that the democrat's self-understanding as a participating citizen be exposed as a myth — a lesson that would be reinforced over and over as the complexities of the new society made politics increasingly bewildering and the efficacy of the typical citizen more and more in doubt. It was also necessary that the myths of the *past* be exploded as well. A movement serious about progress — that believed with John Dewey in the "continuous reconstruction of experience" — could not allow the past to remain unreconstructed. Not only was civic virtue seen to be a myth in the twentieth century, it was also important to show that it had *never* been real.

This task fell on the capable head of Charles A. Beard, a realist political scientist who was arguably this century's most influential American historian as well. Just as Bentley's political science did not permit distinguishing one group from another in respect to their virtue in serving the common good, so Beard's "flat" history showed that the past in this same respect was in no way superior to or even different from the present. His conclusion, traumatic to the patriotic Americans of his day, was that an unsentimental view of the Founding Fathers revealed their feet to be made of some very familiar clay.

The central thesis of Beard's best known and most influential book, *An Economic Interpretation of the Constitution of the United States* (1913), was that the Constitution as it emerged from the convention was essentially an economic and a conservative document, with its political meaning a reflection of the economic interests of those who had framed it. This meant that the Founding Fathers were not disinterested patriots, "working merely under the guidance of abstract principles of political science," but rather, like the politicians of his own day, representatives of "distinct groups whose economic interests they understood and felt in concrete, definite forms through their own personal experience with identical property rights."[30] What is more, since they saw the main threat to their property rights to be the politically volatile common man, the Framers were seen to be fearful of the radical masses, contemptuous of popular judgment, opposed to majority rule — in a word, antidemocratic. In fine, there was a clear link, Beard argued, between the Framers' antidemocratic views, the structure of the Constitution, and their desire to protect their own economic interests.

Academic critics have not dealt gently with Beard's book. Beard's method was seriously faulty, it was said, and he had some of his facts wrong. According to Gordon Wood, it has been "torn to shreds."[31] Much of the criticism, however, seemed to say only that Beard had exaggerated, had only overstated his case; it thus had the no doubt unintended effect of confirming the heart of Beard's thesis: "The Constitution was not *just* an economic document. . . . We would be doing a grave injustice to the political sagacity of the Founding Fathers if we assumed that property or personal gain was their *only* motive. . . . If the members of the Convention were directly interested in the outcome of their work and expected to derive benefits from the establishment of the new system, so *also* did most of the people of the country. . . . Since most of the people were middleclass and had private property, practically *everybody* was interested in the protection of property." Beard had thus failed to see, the critics alleged, that the Founding Fathers were speaking for Americans generally, not just themselves. "A constitution which did not protect property would have been rejected without any question, for the *American people* had fought the Revolution for the preservation of life, liberty, and property."[32] "That personal economic interests were involved is undeniable. Yet the principles they carried with them to Philadelphia would not *all* have fitted in their pocketbooks."[33]

Yet if *some* of those principles were carried to the convention in their pocketbooks, that was good enough in a "realistic" age to establish the "self-interest" of the Framers and, if one were so disposed in an age that was also moralistic, to see such self-interest as tainting their entire enterprise. "To a generation of materialists," wrote Henry Steele Commager, Beard's economic interpretation

> made clear that the stuff of history was material. To a generation disillusioned by the exploitation and ruthlessness of big business, it discovered that the past, too, had been ravaged by exploitation and greed. To a generation that looked with fishy eyes on the claims of Wilsonian idealism and all but rejoiced in their frustration, it suggested that each generation had made similar claims and that all earlier idealisms had been similarly flawed by selfishness and hypocrisy.[34]

Whatever the merits of Beard's analysis, and there was both more and less in Beard's scholarship than his devoted followers and his critics allowed, his characterization of the Framers was the coup de grace for the traditional conception of the American citizen.

For the *citizen*? To the contrary, was not Beard's book a critique of the *Founding Fathers*? And beyond that was it not a covert attack on the entrenched business interests of his day, who had shown themselves to be adept at using the Madisonian Constitution to frustrate citizen-led movements for reform? Had not Beard himself (anachronistically) described the politics of the constitutional era as a struggle between "populism and business"? As a Progressive and a radical, was not Beard against the entrenched conservatives, past and present, and for the popular forces for progress?

True enough. What Beard did, however, was tacitly to deny the possibility of civic or republican virtue as such. If even those fabled American heroes, presented to over a century of American school children as exemplars of all the virtues of the citizen, turned out to be such *ordinary* human beings, what was the point of trying to be anything other than your natural self? The key here, perhaps, is Commager's word "hypocrisy." A. Lawrence Lowell was speaking very much in what was widely assumed to be the spirit of the Founders when he said that the "great statesman" was a kind of moral tutor to the people, appealing always to "higher emotions, to principle, to self-restraint, not to selfishness and appetite." Now, after Beard's realist exposé, it was evident for everyone to see that all the fine talk about principles and self-restraint served only to divert attention from the Founders' own selfish preoccupation with their appetites.

What would have most grieved the Framers of the Constitution, of course, was the attack on their republican virtue implied in the charge that their motives were essentially economic. To the men of Philadelphia this would have signified corruption — the triumph of their private interests over the common good. The unkindest cut of all is that they came out looking very much like one of Madison's factions, "actuated by some common impulse of passion, or of interest, adverse to the rights of other citizens, or to the permanent and aggregate interests of the community."[35] In the language of the Progressive era, which is still our language today, Beard had in effect accused the Founding Fathers of being a "special interest."

Some moral tutors *they* turned out to be! Had the Founding Fathers been honest and realistic, the Progressives have encouraged us to believe, they would have acknowledged frankly and openly that they, like everyone else, were intent on using the *res publica* for their own private and economic advantage. Had they told it like it is, we should suppose, had they been self-aware and up-front about their motives, it might have been unnecessary for Harold Lasswell, that eloquent voice of Progressive realism, to tell us that politics is really only a matter of who gets what, when, and how.

Commager assures us that neither Beard nor his close disciples took "malign satisfaction" in seeing the grand plans of the past revealed as flawed or in seeing "history divested of its heroes, and heroes of their halos."[36] Contrary to his own prescription about what it meant to be scientific, Beard himself was animated in his work, according to Commager, by "patriotism" as well as a "passionate concern" for the truth. "But in those who knew him only through his writings, he encouraged an attitude of iconoclasm and, often, of cynicism."[37]

VI

The difference between Progressive realism and cynicism was at best never easy to see. As the Progressive wisdom has filtered down to our own time, transmitted by legions of teachers, journalists, politicians, novelists, filmmakers, and other shapers of our consciousness, few of whom may ever have heard of Beard or Bentley, much less read their books, we may have lost sight of the difference altogether.

This, it seems to me, is how, finally, we are to understand George Bush's voter — as the apotheosis of this historically transmitted synthesis of realism and cynicism. This commonplace and nonexistent political animal is the Progressive Anti-Myth become the Established Myth of our own time, appearing today as Benthamism *sui generis* transmuted into a politically empty American Dream. A "synthetic–a priori" truth, as philosophers say, neo-Progressive political realism holds that it is both human nature and very American — the way it really is and should be with us — that all men and women, in this case voters, serve only themselves (and their families). It is merely the American Dream the Framers of the Constitution *really* had in mind all along as they laid the foundation for our system of "democratic capitalism," though because of a lot of false consciousness about republicanism they never quite got around to saying so.

After nearly three quarters of a century of being told that the virtues of the traditional citizen are idealistic, moralistic, and the outlook of the self-righteous do-gooder, or worse, illiberal, anti-individualist, or even socialist, we may have landed through "progress" at a point where the current mood makes it possible, even necessary, to regard what was once a priceless possession as empty of any real meaning, as entailing no obligations and promising no political identity — a "citizen" of very easy virtue indeed. What is left of the Progressive crusade on this side of progress has become a holding operation, a kind of neo-Progressive conservatism rooted in the culturally defined "realities" of human nature, whose only political goal is to continue to protect the people against the special interests. Yet everything is now upside down. In his way Bush was making the same assessment of the American voter that Beard made of the Founding Fathers. He was describing a corrupt citizen and a thoroughly corrupt one at that. If the Framers were not statesmen disinterestedly prescribing for the common good, so the average American is not a citizen but only a self-interested voter, using the political system (in this case the presidency), as the Founding Fathers did the Constitution, for private economic benefit.

Unlike Beard, however, Bush is plainly not critical of the object of his analysis, and not only because it would be imprudent to say uncomplimentary things about the people while soliciting their support. The more important reason is that the language of Progressive democracy, which is still our language today, lacks the vocabulary for criticizing the people or even for perceiving flaws in them. For the Progressive-as-crusader "the people" could do no wrong; they *were* the general or public interest against which "special" interests were defined. For the Progressive-as-realist, the scientific analyst of group behavior, there were in the first place no good or bad guys and also no public interest. In both cases there was only power, only the majority—and progress: an endlessly expanding economy and an inexhaustible cornucopia of material blessings, which in the long run made it unnecessary to worry much about who got what, when, or how, or about civic virtue. When progress, "realistically" understood, precludes talk about Croly's "worthier set of men" and concentrates our attention solely on material well-being, the less said about civic virtue the better. This has made it possible for later generations of *liberals* to think of public policy and the polity itself as having no bearing at all on who we are or what kind of human beings we might become, indeed as morally neutral.[38]

In fact, only in old republican terms can the people be corrupt. To say nothing of the Anti-Federalists, even Madison would not hesitate to see in Bush's "people" merely a majority faction, a mass of voters lacking any concern for the common good, interested only in their own advantage. They would be a quiescent majority faction, satisfied, even complacent, to be sure, and thus would fail to pose the kind of political threat Madison feared from the turbulent common man, but they would be a faction nonetheless. And Tocqueville would see in the teeming millions of individuals constituting Bush's polity, all dreaming their own dreams but all dreaming the *same* dream, precisely the ingredients of the majority tyranny he feared.[39]

This accounts in Bush's response to Ferraro for the sort of inverted Progressivism of his attack on the "special interests," those clamorous and easily identifiable groups who have diverted government to their own advantage and against whom the majority of the American people had to be defended by the power of a putatively neutral national administration. To the original Progressives, of course, the "special interests" were the railroads, the oil companies—trusts of every kind: violators all of the American promise, destroyers of competition, stiflers of opportunity, guarantors of inequality, corruptors of politicians. But the "special interests" of our times are very different kinds of groups. They are the groups for whom "progress" remains a chimera—blacks and other minorities, the poor, women, or more broadly, all those unorganized folk lacking wealth, power, and access in a system that will work only on those terms. They are the residual beneficiaries of the lengthening policy and institutional shadow of the New Deal. Unlike "the people" in 1914 or 1984, such groups will never be a majority. Their fate lies with a majority conceived by the wisdom now conventional as purely and simply self-interested, and for that reason, when flattered, incipiently tyrannical.

In the end it is an odd kind of realism that overlooks the wisdom of an imposing line of thinkers with their own reputation for realism who have held that political institutions, including constitutions, must be anchored in the interests, affections, beliefs, and character of the people they govern. Aristotle, Machiavelli, Montesquieu, Rousseau, Burke, Hume, Paine, and Tocqueville, as well as our own Founding Fathers, all argued this point, and all would have declared a society based on the likes of Bush's voter to be impossible.

Contrary to our instincts conditioned by Progressive political realism, candidate Bush, as spokesman for the dominant assumption of our times, is wrong about the American voter and not simply in the obvious sense that typical voters in fact are likely to weigh other factors besides their pocketbooks as they decide how to cast their votes. He is wrong in the more important sense that the entire way of understanding our political life represented by such realism is fundamentally mistaken, and worse, dangerous. No political order could work, our own, perhaps, least of all, if it were composed entirely of the kind of citizen his assessment presupposes. A constitutional democracy committed both to political unity and to social and cultural diversity, yet whose vision is limited to private dreams, is arguably on its way to self-destruction.

The real significance of Mr. Bush's remarks is not that he is talking (mistakenly) *about* real voters but *to* them. It makes a difference how we understand ourselves as a people and as a society, and the way in which we talk to each other about what we basically are will inevitably have consequences. Such prophesies as are generated by our "realism" can be self-fulfilling in ways that are as disastrous as they are real.

NOTES

1. United Press International, 19 September 1984.
2. Associated Press, 30 September 1984.
3. Ibid.
4. Reuters, 8 November 1984. I am indebted to Dale Russakoff of the *Washington Post* for helping me to document the Bush-Ferarro exchange.
5. Alexis de Tocqueville, *Democracy in America*, ed. J. P. Mayer (Garden City, N.Y.: Doubleday, 1969) 2: pt. 2, chap. 2. That individualism (the

"misguided judgment" that society can take care of itself) might degenerate into "egoism" or selfishness (a natural "perversity of the heart") may be said to have been *the* problem of democracy for Tocqueville, and the *Democracy in America* as a whole was an attempt to assay the resources American democracy had to counteract it and thus prevent the rise of a peculiarly democratic form of despotism. One must doubt that Tocqueville himself could have imagined a clearer illustration of the interplay between egoism and individualism than is provided by Bush's voter and conception of the American Dream.

6. Moreover, political opponents of George Bush also must see that it would be inaccurate as well as unjust to suggest that "realism" (as treated here) is all there is to George Bush's outlook. On the contrary, as Michael Novak reminds me, Bush's own life can be seen as an exemplification of just those old republican ideals of citizenship and public service that stand in such sharp contrast to his remarks about voters and the American Dream under examination here. Although in those remarks he articulates clearly what Robert Bellah and his associates call our "first language" of utilitarian individualism, that set of understandings of the human person we modern Americans customarily use to explain and justify our behavior, Bush's actual life is surely an embodiment of our "second language" of republican and biblical individualism, a very different set of understandings generated by Puritanism and early republicanism. See *Habits of the Heart: Individualism and Commitment in American Life* (Berkeley and Los Angeles: University of California Press, 1985). It was exactly this second, earlier, language that *President* Bush used in his Inaugural Address, when he spoke of civic-mindedness, a spirit of "volunteerism," and neighborliness — terms that bespeak a political morality radically at odds with his "realism" of 1984. Alternatively, in the terms elaborated by H. Mark Roelofs, Bush of 1984 was speaking the language of "bourgeois ideology," a set of assumptions describing how self-interested individuals meet and treat one another; *President* Bush, on the other hand, was urging the American individualist to harken to the call of community and the spirit of sacrifice so much a part of "protestant myth." He is the same man, giving voice at different times to the two sides of what Roelofs calls our "schizophrenic" individualism. See *Ideology and Myth in American Politics* (Boston: Little, Brown, 1976), chap. 2. As these analyses indicate, it is seriously to misunderstand American political culture (not to mention George Bush himself) to ask which is the "real" George Bush. The answer, of course, is that both are, even if the Bush of 1984 saw fit to portray his compatriots in only one of these dimensions.

7. Self-interest explains a lot in politics, according to Jane J. Mansbridge, "but the claim that self-interest alone motivates political behavior must be either vacuous, if self-interest can encompass any motive, or false, if self-interest means behavior that consciously intends only self as the beneficiary." "The Rise and Fall of Self-Interest in the Explanation of Polit-

ical Life," in Jane J. Mansbridge, ed., *Beyond Self-Interest* (Chicago: University of Chicago Press, 1990), p. 20.

8. Jean-Jacques Rousseau, *The Social Contract and Discourses*, trans. G. D. H. Cole (New York: E. P. Dutton, 1950), p. 198.

9. Ironically, candidate Ferraro's "idealistic" and complex view that we Americans care about money but also about "each other," considered as a statement capable of being proved or disproved, is in point of fact more realistic than the fashionably tough-minded and simple "realism" of George Bush. It would be easy to show, for example, that countless Americans routinely devote their time and other resources to civic causes on all levels of the American system and that they often explain their so doing by referring simply to a desire to help other people less fortunate than themselves or to a wish to make good things happen for their community. (George Bush's own career, again, is a case in point.) Ferraro is on safe ground in pointing to the well-known charitable instincts of the American people. But what follows from this? It is by no means obvious that "compassion," a prominent Democratic theme in 1984 that seemed to inspire Ferraro's attack on Bush, is necessarily an emotion that citizens in a healthy democracy should feel for each other, especially when it is portrayed, as it was by Mario Cuomo at the convention, as a familial virtue, as a feeling members of the "family of America" should have for one another. Americans have a hard enough time in the closing years of the twentieth century being close to one another as citizens without asking them to love one another as brothers and sisters. Even Rousseau saw "compassion" as a *natural* virtue, which only natural men and women would be expected to feel equally and spontaneously toward their fellow creatures. What a "civilized" and necessarily institutionalized compassion would be like is by no means clear (Rousseau said our natural instincts would be superceded by "justice" in the civil state), and our understanding of the notion is not aided by invoking the metaphor of the family. Still, we Americans *do* care for one another, and it is realistic to say so. For Geraldine Ferraro to have achieved George Bush's level of empirical unrealism, she would have had to say something like, "Of course, we Americans always help others before we help ourselves," an assertion as transparently false as the claim that the only thing that matters in an election is the pocketbook.

10. James Madison, *Federalist* 10.

11. Consider that Michael Dukakis, after quoting John Winthrop on community in his speech accepting his party's nomination at the Democratic National Convention in 1988, ignored that theme thereafter in his campaign and dwelled instead on exactly George Bush's American Dream of 1984.

12. Tocqueville, *Democracy in America*, 2: pt. I, chap. 1.

13. In fact, a society composed wholly or even largely of such voters could conserve nothing—not institutions, not the traditions that give meaning to a nation's politics, not society itself, not even, arguably, the

family Bush invoked to justify his voter's self-interest. We have only to add the universal scramble for power and fear of violent death to this perfected privatism in order to get Hobbes's state of nature, a prospect few conservatives would find attractive. It is only the "conservatism" intrinsic to a thoroughly liberal society, a society that neither fears anarchy nor understands the cultural conditions of social coherence and political viability, that can calmly regard this kind of "pure" individual as existentially real.

14. Quoted in Louis Hartz, *The Liberal Tradition in America* (New York: Harcourt, Brace, 1955), p. 50.

15. Herbert Croly, *The Promise of American Life* (1909; New York: Capricorn Books, 1964), p. 10.

16. Ibid., p. 11.

17. Clinton Rossiter, *The American Presidency* (New York: Signet Key Books, 1956), p. 25, cites the Employment Act of 1946 as providing the first clear recognition of this informal or conventional, i.e., not constitutionally prescribed, function of the president.

18. Theodore J. Lowi, *The End of Liberalism: The Second Republic of the United States*, 2d ed. (New York: W. W. Norton, 1979), chap. 3.

19. Croly, *Promise*, p. 12.

20. Ibid., pp. 31, 35.

21. On the concept of a "political economy" in Hamilton's scheme of things, see Sheldon Wolin, "State and Counter-Revolution," talk at DePauw University (March 1983), and "Reagan Country," *The New York Review of Books* 28 (December 1980): pp. 9–12.

22. Tocqueville, *Democracy in America*, 2: pt. 2, chap. 20.

23. See Sheldon S. Wolin, "From Progress to Modernization: The Conservative Turn," *democracy* 3 (Fall 1983): 9–21.

24. In seeming to portray the Progressives alternatively as crusaders and scientific realists, I do not wish to suggest that particular figures in the movement were necessarily or exclusively either one or the other. On the contrary, as Crick's account suggests, the two tendencies in Progressivism I distinguish with these labels were both more or less articles of faith to most of the leading figures of the day. (See Bernard Crick, *The American Science of Politics* [Westport, Conn: Greenwood Press, 1959], pp. 74, 124.) John Dewey, who above all devoted himself to overcoming such "dualisms," who indeed defined "democracy" and "science" as complementary ways of thinking and acting, is an obvious case in point. Dewey's attempted synthesis notwithstanding, Progressive idealism and realism, I think we can now see, were contradictory impulses with very different implications, both destructive, for a conception of democratic citizenship.

25. Jefferson is surely one of the main sources of American liberalism, as David Greenstone argues, but his contribution to American democracy is less clear. For all Jefferson's legendary trust in the political capacities of the common man and despite his insistence that citizens be "participators in the government of affairs," Jefferson's "pursuit of happiness" is notoriously

ambiguous. It is as much a prescription for the privatism of Bush's American Dream as it is for republican virtue. See Hannah Arendt, *On Revolution* (New York: Viking Press, 1965), pp. 124–29. Cf. Joyce Appleby, "Jefferson: A Political Reappraisal," *democracy* 3 (Fall 1983): 139–145. Although "old republicanism" surely did emphasize public duties, Greenstone suggests that Adams, and not Jefferson, is the more faithful transmitter of that part of the republican persuasion. See his discussion of Jefferson's ambivalence about public service, p. 25.

26. John Dewey, *Democracy and Education* (New York: Macmillan, 1916), p. 87.

27. Although in what follows I concentrate on the new political science, it should be said that all the newly professionalized social sciences, as well as the (muckraking) journalism of the day, contributed to our present understanding that "reality" is always mundane and always at odds with what Lowell called the "higher emotions." In establishing this almost undisputed "insider's" wisdom, the discipline of economics was surely not less important than the new political science, as is suggested by the ease with which the purely self-interested voter is seen as the political counterpart of the "economic man" of textbook lore. "Possibly the worst single contribution of the economics profession to the understanding of political society," writes Robert Kuttner, "is the tautological and straitened attempt to reduce all public-spiritedness or altruism to merely an odd, masochistic special case of egoistic utility-maximization. As Steven Kelman has observed, an ethic of public service is vital to a democratic system of government. When everything is reduced to a private, profit-maximizing transaction, that ethic is diminished." "False Profit: The Perils of Privatization," *New Republic* 200 (6 February 1989): 23. For a wide-ranging critique of this tendency in American social science and especially in political science, see Mansbridge, ed., *Beyond Self-Interest*, cited above, n. 7.

28. Quoted in Crick, *American Science of Politics*, p. 75.

29. Quoted, ibid., p. 118.

30. Charles A. Beard, *An Economic Interpretation of the Constitution of the United States* (New York: Macmillan, 1929), p. 73.

31. Gordon S. Wood, "Democracy and the Constitution," in Robert A. Goldwin and William A. Schambra, eds., *How Democratic Is the Constitution?* (Washington, D.C.: American Enterprise Institute for Policy Research, 1980), p. 3.

32. Robert E. Brown, *Charles Beard and the Constitution: A Critical Analysis of "An Economic Interpretation of the Constitution"* (Princeton, N.J.: Princeton University Press, 1956), pp. 197–98. Emphasis added.

33. Edmund S. Morgan, *The Birth of the Republic—1763–1789* (Chicago: University of Chicago Press, 1956), p. 132. Emphasis added.

34. Henry Steele Commager, *The American Mind: An Interpretation of American Thought and Character Since the 1880s* (New Haven, Conn.: Yale University Press, 1950), p. 307.

35. Madison, *Federalist* 10.

36. Commager, *American Mind*, p. 307.

37. Ibid., p. 308.

37. See Michael J. Sandel, "Morality and the Liberal Ideal," *New Republic* 190 (7 May 1984): 15-17. With "liberal," the dreaded "L" word, increasingly in disfavor as a label, we must note the irony in the alternative some erstwhile liberals have chosen to describe themselves and their program. It is, of course, "progressive."

39. The importance of "caring for one another," Tocqueville might have lectured Geraldine Ferraro and even more so George Bush, was not for the sake of "compassion" but to guarantee that American civil society would not become a collection of disconnected, isolated individuals, ripe for "administrative" despotism — that it would continue to provide barriers against majority tyranny and the kind of despotism, itself a product of "progress," that democracies had most to fear. This requires not welfare programs (though it does not preclude them) but democratic political action and the sort of "good life" a rightly conceived democracy can nurture.

INDEX